The British Empire
The End of Colonialism

by William W. Lace

Lucent Books, San Diego, CA

Titles in the History's Great Defeats series include:

The Aztecs: End of a Civilization
The British Empire: The End of Colonialism
The Cold War: Collapse of Communism
The Third Reich: Demise of the Nazi Dream

Library of Congress Cataloging-in-Publication Data

Lace, William W.
    The British Empire: the end of colonialism / by William W. Lace
        p.   cm. — (History's great defeats)
    Includes bibliographical references (p.) and index.
    Summary: Examines the events leading to expansion of the British Empire and the variety of reasons for its eventual decline in the twentieth century.
    ISBN 1-56006-683-0 (lib. bdg. : alk. paper)
    1. Great Britain—Colonies—History—20th century—Juvenile literature. 2. Postcolonialism—Commonwealth countries—History— Juvenile literature. 3. Decolonization—History—20th century— Juvenile literature. 4. Commonwealth countries—History—Juvenile literature. [1. Great Britain—Colonies—History. 2. Commonwealth countries—History.] I. Title. II. Series.

DA16 .L23   2000
909'.0971241—dc21
                                                        99-057228

Copyright © 2000 by Lucent Books, Inc.
P.O. Box 289011
San Diego, CA 92198-9011
Printed in the U.S.A.

Table of Contents

Foreword

H ISTORY IS FILLED with tales of dramatic encounters that sealed the fates of empires or civilizations, changing them or causing them to disappear forever. One of the best known events began in 334 B.C., when Alexander, king of Macedonia, led his small but formidable Greek army into Asia. In the short span of only ten years, he brought Persia, the largest empire the world had yet seen, to its knees, earning him the nickname forever after associated with his name—"the Great." The demise of Persia, which at its height stretched from the shores of the Mediterranean Sea in the west to the borders of India in the east, was one of history's most stunning defeats. It occurred primarily because of some fatal flaws in the Persian military system, disadvantages the Greeks had exploited before, though never as spectacularly as they did under Alexander.

First, though the Persians had managed to conquer many peoples and bring huge territories under their control, they had failed to create an individual fighting man who could compare with the Greek hoplite. A heavily armored infantry soldier, the hoplite fought in a highly effective and lethal battlefield formation—the phalanx. Possessed of better armor, weapons, and training than the Persians, Alexander's soldiers repeatedly crushed their Persian opponents. Second, the Persians for the most part lacked generals of the caliber of their Greek counterparts. And when Alexander invaded, Persia had the added and decisive disadvantage of facing one of the greatest generals of all time. When the Persians were defeated, their great empire was lost forever.

Other world powers and civilizations have fallen in a like manner. They have succumbed to some combination of inherent fatal flaws or

4

disadvantages, to political and/or military mistakes, and even to the personal failings of their leaders.

Another of history's great defeats was the sad demise of the North American Indian tribes at the hands of encroaching European civilization from the sixteenth to nineteenth centuries. In this case, all of the tribes suffered from the same crippling disadvantages. Among the worst, they lacked the great numbers, the unity, and the advanced industrial and military hardware possessed by the Europeans. Still another example, one closer to our own time, was the resounding defeat of Nazi Germany by the Allies in 1945, which brought World War II, the most disastrous conflict in history, to a close. Nazi Germany collapsed for many reasons. But one of the most telling was that its leader, Adolf Hitler, sorely underestimated the material resources and human resolve of the Allies, especially the United States. In the end, Germany was in a very real sense submerged by a massive and seemingly relentless tidal wave of Allied bombs, tanks, ships, and soldiers.

Seen in retrospect, a good many of the fatal flaws, drawbacks, and mistakes that caused these and other great defeats from the pages of history seem obvious. It is only natural to wonder why, in each case, the losers did not realize their limitations and/or errors sooner and attempt to avert disaster. But closer examination of the events, social and political trends, and leading personalities involved usually reveals that complex factors were at play. Arrogance, fear, ignorance, stubbornness, innocence, and other attitudes held by nations, peoples, and individuals often colored and shaped their reactions, goals, and strategies. And it is both fascinating and instructive to reconstruct how such attitudes, as well as the fatal flaws and mistakes themselves, contributed to the losers' ultimate demise.

Each volume in Lucent Books' *History's Great Defeats* series is designed to provide the reader with diverse learning tools for exploring the topic at hand. Each well-informed, clearly written text is supported and enlivened by substantial quotes by the actual people involved, as well as by later historians and other experts; and these primary and secondary sources are carefully documented. Each volume also supplies the reader with an extensive Works Consulted list, guiding him or her to further research on the topic. These and other research tools, including glossaries and time lines, afford the reader a thorough understanding of how and why one of history's most decisive defeats occurred and how these events shaped our world.

Land of Hope and Glory

O N DECEMBER 6, 1922, in the chilly courtyard of Dublin Castle, two men stood at attention—the Lord Lieutenant of Ireland, representative of Great Britain, and Michael Collins, representative of the new Irish government. As they saluted, a military band blared forth "God Save the King." Slowly, the Union Jack, the flag of Great Britain and the worldwide symbol of the British Empire, was lowered—never to rise again after flying above the castle for more than four centuries. In its place, a new flag was raised—the green, white, and orange banner of the Irish Free State.

Great Britain's initial colony, Ireland, had become the first since the thirteen American colonies to break free. It was the beginning of the end for the vast British Empire.

In 1817, London journalist John Wilson had written, "The sun never sets upon the Union Jack."[1] In other words, the British Empire was so widespread that, as the earth turned on its axis during a twenty-four-hour period, the sun was always shining on a British possession somewhere. Wilson's boast was even more true a century later. In the 1920s, as a result of World War I, Britain controlled one-fourth of the world's land area and more than one-fourth of the population. Britain's bewildering variety of colonies, protectorates, possessions, dominions, and mandates was so numerous that one colonial secretary (the top government official in charge of the empire) complained that he had to "keep looking up the damned places on the map."[2]

6

Wider and Wider

To generations of Britons, it must have seemed that their empire would grow and endure forever. At the opening of the twentieth century, they proudly sang the patriotic hymn by Edward Elgar:

Land of hope and glory, mother of the free
How shall we extol thee, who art born of thee?
Wider still and wider shall thy bounds be set;
God who made thee mighty, make thee mightier yet.[3]

And yet, as the century came to an end, the empire had all but vanished, and Britain had been relegated to a secondary role among world powers.

What had happened? The key to the decline of the British Empire was that, although Britain appeared in control of its own destiny and that of most of the world, it was not as mighty as Elgar's hymn would suggest. As the empire grew, the problems of holding it together grew in proportion. Several factors, most of them external, began to tug at the structure until it finally collapsed under its own weight.

To begin with, there was the changing geopolitical landscape. Britannia might have "ruled the waves" in the early 1800s, but new rivals arose to challenge its supremacy: Germany in Europe, Japan in the Pacific, and the United States in the Western Hemisphere.

The Cost of Warfare

Warfare was another major factor. The British could claim victory in the Boer War of 1899–1902, World War I, and World War II, but they were so weakened that their ability to rule the empire was lessened.

Economics also played a large part in the decline of the empire. One of the major reasons for having colonies had been to benefit the mother country economically. The colonies produced raw materials for British industries and also served as markets for the goods produced by those industries. Gradually, however, the cost of the empire became greater than its benefits. That cost became even greater because of events such as the Great Depression of the 1930s.

Perhaps the most dramatic factor was the worldwide movement in the twentieth century toward self-determination for all people. The era of the "white man's" domination was ending. Leaders such as

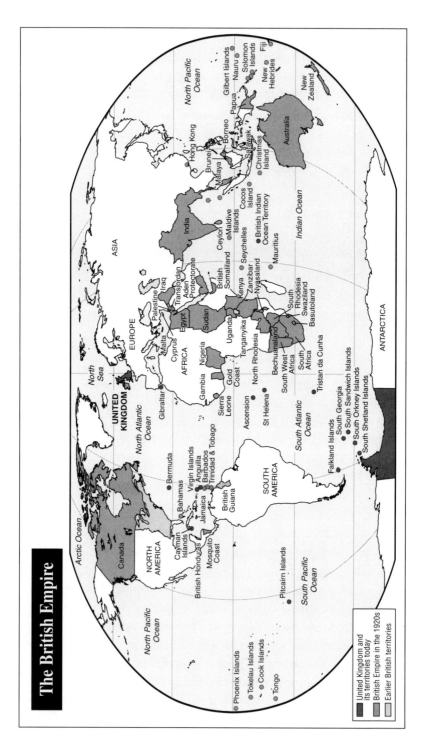

The British Empire

Mohandas Gandhi in India struck the sparks that ignited blazes of nationalism throughout the empire—too many blazes, eventually, for Britain to extinguish.

The final factor, one that probably stemmed from the rest, was that the British seemed to lose the spirit that had driven them to build their empire. Fewer young men were willing to suffer the hardships of colonial life. There was also less enthusiasm for "enlightening" the native people.

As a result of these major factors, the British Empire disappeared, bit by bit. In the late 1960s British troops worldwide were brought home, except for a tiny garrison in Hong Kong that would remain until 1997. An era in world history had ended. The basic cause of the empire's dissolution was reflected on November 29, 1967, when British troops left what on the next day would become the People's Republic of South Yemen. As the troops marched toward waiting airplanes, the Royal Marine band struck up a once-popular music hall tune, "Fings Ain't Wot They Used to Be."

Chapter 1

Sunrise

THE BRITISH EMPIRE WAS not a product of conquest as much as it was a haphazard outcome of circumstances, some beyond British control. It was not a product of orderly growth or consistent government policy but was, rather, a confusing jumble of colonies, possessions, protectorates, and mandates that had little in common with one another except a vague allegiance to the British Crown. The empire, mightiest in world history, was assembled as much by accident as by design, and it finally reached a point where it almost took on a life of its own. By the time the British began wishing to rid themselves of the burdens of empire, it had become an economic and political necessity. They were in the same position as a person who succeeds in riding a tiger only to find no easy way off.

Historians have called the British Empire that withered away during the twentieth century the "Second British Empire," as opposed to the original colonies established during the 1600s. Britain had gotten off to a late start in the race for overseas colonies sparked by Christopher Columbus's voyages in the late 1400s. It was not until 1607 that the first British colony, Virginia, was established on the eastern coast of North America, soon to be followed by its twelve neighbors.

The British established a foothold in Canada in 1610 with a colony in Newfoundland and one in the Caribbean in 1623 with the settlement of the island of Barbados. At first, Britain was restricted in both areas since France was the dominant power in Canada and Spain controlled most of Latin America. As Spain's power diminished, however, more islands, such as Jamaica, Bermuda, and the

Bahamas, came under British rule, and most of French Canada was taken over in 1763 as a result of the French and Indian War.

The First Empire

These American colonies, along with Ireland, formed the "First British Empire." Except for the West Indies, where native labor was used, the empire was made up of true colonies, ones to which thousands of native Britons moved in search of new lives. Later, this would also be true of British colonies in Australia, South Africa, and New Zealand, although in the case of Australia, a penal colony, the immigration was often involuntary.

This First British Empire effectively ended with the revolt of the thirteen North American colonies and the resulting independence of the United States. Although some expansion continued in Canada, Britain's dream of dominating the Americas could no longer be realized.

Other conquests, however, were not far off. The defeat of Napoleon Bonaparte and the French in 1815 left Britain the world's dominant power and opened the doors to the spread of the Second British Empire. This collection of possessions was very different from the former colonies in that they consisted not of British

---

 ## The Justifications for Empire

To many Britons, imperialism was much more than a contest to see which country could grab up more colonies and make more profits from them. They believed that in expanding their colonial empire the British were fulfilling a racial destiny. Lord Milner, the high commissioner of South Africa, said (as quoted in *The British Imperial Experience* by Robert A. Huttenback):

> Imperialism as a political doctrine has been represented as something tawdry and superficial. In reality it has all the depth and comprehensiveness of a religious faith. Its significance is moral even more than material. It is a mistake to think of it as principally concerned with "painting the map red" [the traditional British color]. There is quite enough painted red already. It is not a question of a couple of hundred thousand square miles more or less. It is a question of preserving the unity of a great race, of enabling it, by maintaining that unity, to develop freely on its own line, and to continue to fulfill its distinctive mission in the world.

---

colonists but of native peoples governed by British officials who were backed up by the British military.

India in 1805

The centerpiece of the British Empire was India, sometimes called the "jewel in the crown." India was by far the richest part of the empire, providing the mother country with raw materials and then serving as a major market for the products of those materials. It was so vital to Britain's national interest that many of the other colonies were obtained for the sole purpose of protecting it. India's importance dwarfed that of the rest of the empire to such an extent that it was included in Queen Victoria's official title along with Great Britain and Ireland.

Turning Toward India

When the British East India Company was founded in 1600, the principal objective was not India but the spice-rich East Indies. The Dutch, however, wanted a monopoly on trade there and expelled the British in 1623. The British then turned to India, establishing coastal trading centers at Surat, Bombay, Calcutta, and Madras.

First Portugal and then France were Britain's chief rivals in India. The British got the upper hand in 1757, however, when Robert Clive, an official of the East India Company, engineered a revolt in the state of Bengal. He defeated the native ruler at the Battle of Plassey and put his own candidate on the throne. Four years later the French were defeated at Pondicherry. Britain was now the dominant European power, and over the next century the East India Company came to control most of India, governing either outright or through puppet native princes.

A mutiny among native soldiers in Bengal in 1857 led to a widespread revolt against the British. After two years of bitter fighting, British control was restored and the line of the Mughal kings, who had ruled in name only, came to an end. The most important outcome of the revolt was that Britain assumed direct control of India; this control was centered in a British viceroy, a direct representative of the Crown. The era of the British *raj,* the Hindu word for "reign," had arrived.

India had become Britain's richest possession and its largest trading partner, furnishing cotton and other raw materials and becoming a huge market for British products. One viceroy, Marquess Curzon, called it "the miracle of the world."[4] Britain was compelled to protect its investment in India. The result was most of the rest of the British Empire.

The Cape Colony

Protecting India also meant protecting routes from Britain to India. Until the mid-1900s, the easiest way for people and goods to make the journey was by sea, and the easiest sea route, until the 1869 opening of the Suez Canal in Egypt, was around the Cape of Good Hope on the southern tip of Africa. The Dutch had established a colony on

---

 ## The Black Hole of Calcutta

Popular support in Britain for the military campaign in the Indian state of Bengal in 1757 was fueled by the story of the "Black Hole of Calcutta." The story was held up as an example of the barbarity and cruelty of the native rulers and thus of the necessity to impose British rule.

In June 1756, the British East India Company, anticipating a war against the French, began fortifying a small town it had built near the city of Calcutta. The local *nwab,* or ruler, Siraj-ud-Dawlah, objected and overran the settlement. The British, led by John Z. Holwell, surrendered.

On the night of June 20, according to Holwell, 146 British men, women, and children were put in a single cell measuring eighteen feet by fourteen feet and having only two small windows. Because of the crowding and the stifling heat, Holwell reported, 123 people died before they were released the next morning. The cell became known as the Black Hole, and the incident fueled a British desire for revenge.

Subsequent historical research by both Indian and British scholars indicates that, although the incident did take place, reports of it were highly exaggerated. Indian historian Brijen Gupta's 1959 study reported that the number of Europeans locked up that night was sixty-four and that forty-three died. Furthermore, it is now doubtful that Siraj-ud-Dawlah even knew about the incident at the time.

the cape in 1653, but the British captured it in 1806 to act as a way station on the route to India. Later, South Africa would become extremely valuable in its own right as a source of gold and diamonds.

From South Africa, the British expanded northward, taking in Bechuanaland and the huge area that would become Southern Rhodesia and Northern Rhodesia. The latter seizure came at the instigation of Cecil Rhodes, an adventurer for whom the colonies were later named. Rhodes had convinced the British South Africa Company that there were immense profits to be made from mining. The British incorporation of southern Africa was completed in 1902 with the conquest of the Orange Free State and the Transvaal from the Boers, descendants of the Dutch settlers.

The sea voyage to India became easier with the opening of the Suez Canal, which was controlled jointly by the British and French. Britain became concerned that instability in the Egyptian government might close the waterway, and in 1882 it invaded Egypt and took control of the canal. Although Egypt never officially became a British possession, British troops kept order and dictated the country's foreign policy and defense.

Protecting Egypt

If Egypt was necessary to protect India, then other acquisitions were needed to protect Egypt. Since Egypt was almost totally dependent on the Nile River, the British thought it best to control the Nile south of the Egyptian border. Thus Uganda was occupied in 1888 and Sudan ten years later. Since a railroad from the coast to Uganda was desirable, neighboring Kenya was made British to furnish an overland route. To facilitate shipping to Kenya, the off-coast island of Zanzibar flew the Union Jack.

After World War I, another large chunk of Africa came Britain's way. With the defeat of Germany, its colonies were divided between Britain and France; Britain gained South-West Africa, the Cameroons, Togoland, and Tanganyika. The acquisition of Tanganyika made it possible for a person to travel the forty-six hundred miles overland from Cape Town on the Cape of Good Hope to Alexandria on the Mediterranean without leaving the British Empire.

Most of the British possessions on the west coast of Africa belonged more to the First British Empire than to the second. Gambia,

Cecil Rhodes: Arch Imperialist

Some Britons excused empire building on the grounds that it brought civilization to the "savages" of Africa and Asia. No one was more extreme in his views than Cecil Rhodes, a wealthy diamond miner who wanted to extend British rule over most of Africa and did not care how he did it, employing bribery, trickery, and brute force.

Rhodes's objective was the large area north of South Africa known as Zambezia. In 1888 he tricked Lobengula, king of Zambezia's dominant tribe, the Matabele, into signing a document he claimed only gave him mining rights in the area. Actually, lured by the promise of money, rifles and ammunition, and an armed steamboat, Lobengula had virtually signed away his kingdom. Rhodes promptly convinced the British government to charter a company, with himself at the head, to open the area that eventually bore his name—Rhodesia. A capital city was founded and named Salisbury after the current British prime minister. Lobengula never got his steamboat.

Motivated by profits, business magnate Cecil Rhodes used whatever means possible to extend British rule throughout Africa.

When Lobengula realized what had happened, he attempted to regain control. In 1893 he ordered raids against British outposts, and some settlers were killed. It was just the excuse Rhodes needed. British troops were called in and a short, sharp war was fought; the Matabele, armed mostly with spears, had no chance against the British machine guns.

As a result, the entire area, as Rhodes wished, became a British protectorate. Rhodes died in 1902 and was buried on a rocky hilltop in Rhodesia. Much of his fabulous wealth went to establish the famous Rhodes Scholarship at Oxford University in Britain.

Sierra Leone, the Gold Coast, and outposts in Nigeria originally supported the slave trade. After the abolition of slavery, they served as the centers of the successful British attempt to halt the exportation of slaves from West Africa.

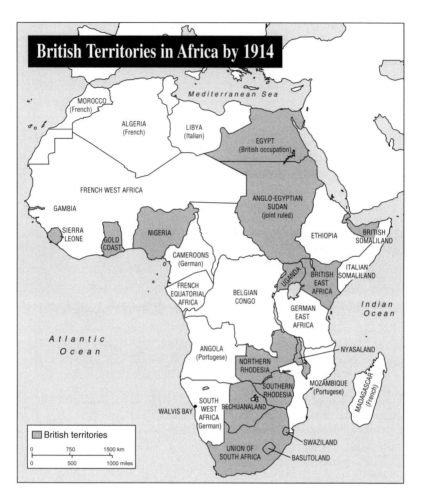

British Territories in Africa by 1914

Indeed, the British saw their role throughout Africa as bringing civilization to savages. Lord Lugard, an official in East Africa, wrote,

> Not against the slave-trade alone are our efforts needed. . . . The *Pax Britannia* which shall stop this lawless raiding and this constant inter-tribal war will be the greatest blessing that Africa has known since the Flood."[5]

The Gulf Colonies

Control of the Suez Canal gave Britain only partial control of the shorter sea route to India. After passage through the Red Sea, shipping had to go through the narrow Bab el Mandeb Strait before going on to the Gulf of Aden and the Indian Ocean. To ensure that the strait remained open, the British took over what later became British Somaliland on the African shore in 1884. They had already colonized Aden on the southern tip of the Arabian peninsula in 1839. Aden, along with Qatar and Kuwait in the Persian Gulf, was ruled from India, not London—another example of the importance of India.

The need to protect and defend India was felt as far away as the Mediterranean. The islands of Minorca and Malta had been British since 1708 and 1800, respectively, but additional protection for Egypt was realized in 1878 with the annexation of the much larger island of Cyprus.

The end of World War I gave Britain control over parts of the Middle East as well as Africa. With the breakup of the Turkish Empire, the British were given "mandates" to rule Palestine, Transjordan (present-day Jordan), and Iraq. The old excuse of protection for Egypt and the route to India was given, but the British now had a far better reason for a presence in the area—oil.

A French colonist stands with native Senegalese workers at a steam engine plant in this 1885 photograph. Europeans saw it as their duty to bring civilization to the natives.

Britain continued to dominate the Middle East into the 1930s despite having made vague promises to both the Arabs and Jews during World War I about granting full independence. Those promises were not kept, and the British sought to retain control of the area by taking advantage of the conflict between the Arabs and Jews, playing one side against the other. As the conflict escalated, Palestine provided some of the ugliest episodes in the history of the British Empire, including the imprisoning of women and children and the torture of those suspected of terrorist activities.

Possessions in Africa and the Middle East protected the approach to India from the west, but Britain had to protect its crown jewel to the east as well, particularly once the United States and Japan emerged as world powers. The reasons for the growth of the British Empire in the Pacific Ocean, however, dealt mostly with domestic politics and economics.

Outlets for Emigration

The loss of the North American colonies in 1776 and a phenomenal growth in the British birthrate in the early 1800s meant that Britain needed additional outlets for emigration. Australia and New Zealand were the primary outlets that were developed.

Australia, at first primarily a penal colony, soon began to attract settlers from Britain. The original colony, New South Wales, was joined by central Australia and Tasmania in 1825, and the western third was added in 1829. The Anglo settlers completely dominated the aborigines, using them chiefly for what amounted to slave labor. One prosperous rancher said that "there was no more harm in shooting a native than in shooting a dog."[6] Australia quickly became a commercial success, furnishing high-quality wool to British mills.

Britain reaped similar economic benefits from New Zealand, to which Scottish sheep farmers emigrated by the thousands in the 1800s after it became a British colony in 1788. British settlers there had a far more difficult time subduing the native population than did those in Australia. The New Zealand Maoris, proud, warlike, and fiercely independent, were subdued only after almost a hundred years of sporadic fighting.

Even though they had considerable native populations, Australia and New Zealand were considered "white" portions of the empire

Britain's colony, New South Wales, attracted British emigrants, who often settled as sheep farmers.

and, along with Canada and South Africa, eventually were accorded status as dominions rather than colonies. They were largely self-governing and were expected to come to the aid of Britain only in times of war. Britain, on the other hand, was expected to use its military to protect the interest of the dominions.

Singapore

Although they had Australia and New Zealand, the British needed another strong outpost east of India for protection of the sea lanes. It was furnished in 1819 when Sir Stamford Raffles of the East India Company leased the island of Singapore off the southern tip of Malaya. It would thrive not only as a naval base but as a center of commerce for the entire South Pacific. Eventually, the British also gained control of the entire Malay Peninsula to the north, thereby also dominating the world production of rubber.

One of the dreams of British imperialists was to add China to Queen Victoria's crown. They never realized that dream, but they did manage to add the commercial center of Hong Kong, on the southwest coast of China, to the empire, obtaining it on a long-term lease.

Though one of the empire's smallest pieces, Hong Kong was one of the richest, and also one of the last to be lost.

East of Malaya and governed from Singapore were the colonies of North Borneo, Brunei, and Sarawak. The first two were founded by a private company in London. Sarawak was unusual: It had been carved out of the jungle by a British subject, James Brooke, acting

The White Raja of Sarawak

Many men governed colonies throughout the long history of the British Empire, but only one—James Brooke—was able to found a dynasty. Sarawak, on the northern coast of Borneo on the South China Sea, was considered part of the empire but was ruled as a kingdom by Brooke and his family for more than one hundred years.

Born in India, Brooke served as a soldier for the British East India Company before setting out on his own as a trader in the 1830s, sailing the

James Brooke ruled as the "white raja" of Sarawak for nearly thirty years.

East Indies in an armed ship purchased with an inheritance. In 1839 he offered his services to the sultan of Brunei, who was at war with rebel tribes in Sarawak, part of his territory.

When the rebellion was crushed in 1841, the grateful sultan made Brooke raja, or prince, of Sarawak. Five years later he was given the title in perpetuity, meaning it could be handed down through his family.

When Brooke died in 1868, the title went to his nephew Charles Anthony Johnson Brooke, who did much to improve the lives of the natives, learning their language and customs. He died in 1917, and his oldest son, Charles Vyner de Windt Brooke, became the third "white raja." He modernized the country, which grew in wealth after World War I by exporting rubber and oil.

In 1941, on the one hundredth anniversary of the family's rule, Charles Vyner de Windt Brooke proclaimed a constitution and announced his intention to make Sarawak self-governing. World War II intervened, but on July 1, 1946, Brooke—despite heated opposition from other members of the family—ceded Sarawak to Britain and ended the dynasty. Sarawak, in turn, was ceded to Malaysia in 1963.

entirely on his own in 1841. Although its foreign affairs were eventually run by Britain, Brooke and his descendants ruled Sarawak almost like kings. It gained independence only in 1963.

The other large British possessions in the South Pacific were on the island of New Guinea. Papua, the southeastern portion, was taken over jointly in 1907 by Britain and Australia and administered by the Australian government. The southwestern portion, British New Guinea, came as a result of the defeat of Germany in World War I.

The Worldwide Empire

There was more, much more, to the British Empire. There were British Honduras in Central America and British Guiana in South America, plus a dozen Caribbean islands. There were the tiny island of Helgoland off the coast of Denmark and St. Helena in the South Atlantic, famous as Napoleon's final place of exile. There were Burma and more than a hundred Pacific islands, as rich and important as the Solomons and the Fiji Islands and as insignificant as Pitcairn Island, inhabited mostly by descendants of the sailors who had sought refuge there in the *HMS Bounty* after they had seized the ship in the mutiny made famous later in books and motion pictures.

The height of the British Empire was reached in the years between World Wars I and II, but the forces that would lead to its decline had been in motion for decades and were just beginning to be felt. Still, the empire was staggering in its scope, and it is no wonder that British children at the start of the twentieth century learned as part of an alphabet song,

C is for Colonies
Rightly we boast,
That of all the great nations
Great Britain has most.[7]

The Changing
Chapter 2 World Order

I N THE MID-1800s the people of Britain could confidently sing the
song written a century earlier by James Thompson and Thomas
Arne that had become almost a second national anthem:

Rule Britannia!
Britannia rules the waves.
Britons never, never, never
Shall be slaves.[8]

After the defeat of Napoleon Bonaparte and France in 1815, Great
Britain, indeed, was without a serious world rival.

Over the next century, however, the geopolitical situation
changed dramatically. An invigorated France expanded its colonial
empire. Germany and Russia challenged British superiority. Japan
became the first Asian power, and the United States took on more of
an international role. As early as 1885, the *Pall Mall Gazette* be-
moaned the trend:

Our old position is lost—irrevocably. . . . In times past . . .
we did what we pleased, where we pleased, and as we
pleased. . . . All that has changed. Europe has overflowed
into Africa, Asia, America, Australasia and the Pacific. At
every turn we are confronted with the gunboats, the sea lairs,
or the colonies of jealous and eager rivals. . . . The world is
filling up around us.[9]

To resist the challenge, Great Britain felt forced to expand its empire.
The result was an empire that stretched far beyond the British capabilities of holding on to it.

France

France was Britain's ancient enemy. The two countries had been at war on and off for five hundred years. Although the Napoleonic Wars (1793–1815) were their last full-scale conflicts, the rivalry continued throughout the 1800s, especially in Africa.

During the first half of the century, France established itself as a power in North Africa. The British were not especially concerned since the only sea route to India at the time was around the southern tip of the continent. The situation changed dramatically when the French built the Suez Canal.

France's opening of the Suez Canal in 1869 (pictured) threatened Britain's position as the dominant power in Africa.

The British had not wanted the canal built. They were content to dominate the sea lanes around the Cape of Good Hope. When the canal opened in 1869, however, it posed a threat. France was now closer to India than Britain, and steps had to be taken.

In 1875 the British bought a 44-percent interest in the canal from the bankrupt khedive, or ruler, of Egypt and shared control with the French. This arrangement lasted until 1882 when the Egyptians rioted against the Europeans. France pulled out, leaving Britain to quell the uprising and take sole control of the canal. The entire Egyptian episode, which Britain had not sought, served to embroil it in a series of costly Middle Eastern ventures.

The French also provoked a British response in the Sudan, immediately to the south of Egypt and technically under Egyptian control. Britain had put down a native revolt there in 1885, but in 1895 the French sent an expedition to Fashoda on the upper reaches of the Nile River. They believed a dam could be built that could threaten Egypt's water supply and perhaps force the British to share control of Egypt or abandon the country altogether.

Showdown at Fashoda

Britain reacted by sending an army under Sir Herbert Kitchener to conquer the Sudan and take it from its native ruler. The conflict lasted two years and ended with a British victory at Omdurman. Kitchener proceeded to the outpost at Fashoda and demanded that the French haul down their flag. The French commander, Captain Jean-Baptiste Marchand, at first refused, and the two countries prepared for war. The French military, however, was not strong enough to challenge Britain, and Marchand withdrew. The British had won, but they now had yet another possession that took money from the treasury because of the stationing of troops there yet provided little in the way of trade or raw materials.

Less serious but still costly to Britain was the rivalry with France in West Africa. Britain had enjoyed an informal relationship with the native rulers of Nigeria and had a virtual monopoly on palm oil. In 1884, however, France began making treaties with local tribal chiefs in an attempt to control the upper Niger River.

By 1898 Britain had realized the threat and sent a small army to Nigeria to confront the French. Eventually, the matter was settled

By Hook or Crook

As European powers vied with one another for colonies in Africa, they used every means possible to achieve their ends. The favorite tactic was to make treaties with the natives. Often, the native chiefs had no idea they were giving away their authority. The pact signed by King Lobengula of Zambezia, for instance, was supposedly a mining agreement. Later, when his country had been taken over by the British, Lobengula complained that he thought the white men only wanted to dig a big hole in the ground.

When diplomacy or trickery failed, however, the British and other European countries resorted to force. As a British poem popular before the Crimean War said,

> We don't want to fight, but, by Jingo, if we do,
> We've got the ships, we've got the guns, we've got the money, too.

Most of the fighting, however, was against the natives, who, although numerous and brave, could not withstand modern weapons. The most effective of these weapons was the Maxim gun, the first true machine gun. Even though they were only a handful against a horde, the British soldiers could take comfort in the rhyme

> Whatever happens we have got
> The Maxim gun and they have not.

The deadliness of the Maxim gun made a deep impression on the native tribes. In the 1970s, a very old man of the Ndebele tribe was asked to explain his unusual name, Zigga-Zigga. It was the sound made by the Maxim gun, he explained, and thus a name of great power.

---

diplomatically. The British took full possession of Nigeria, and the French were given concessions elsewhere.

Germany

Until 1871 Germany was a patchwork of independent states, none of which had colonial aspirations. Even after its unification, Chancellor Otto von Bismarck exclaimed, "I will have no colonies. For Germany to possess colonies would be like a poverty-stricken Polish nobleman acquiring a silk sable coat when he needed shirts."[10]

Barely more than a decade later, Bismarck changed his tune. German agents quietly began concluding treaties with native chiefs. In 1884 Germany announced that it had annexed South-West Africa, Togoland, and the Cameroons in Western Africa. The next year a

By the end of the nineteenth century, Germany had joined Britain and France in colonizing Africa. Here, native workers construct a road in German-colonized Togoland in about 1910.

surprised Britain learned that Germany had taken possession of Tanganyika in East Africa. Furthermore, the Germans encouraged Belgium to establish itself in the Congo.

Outwardly, the British reaction was one of calm. "If Germany is to become a colonizing power," said Prime Minister William Gladstone, "all I can say is 'God speed her!'"[11] Privately, the British were worried. Two Boer republics—the Transvaal and the Orange Free State—lay northeast of Britain's Cape Colony, and the Boers and Germans were on good terms. Working together, they could isolate the British on the southern tip of the continent.

Convinced of their danger by Cecil Rhodes, a millionaire South African miner and adventurer, the British seized Bechuanaland, just to the north of the cape, in 1885. They then moved into the area north of Bechuanaland and took possession of what would become Rhodesia. Rhodes had predicted that great wealth would come to Britain as a result of the new territories. The wealth failed to materialize, and Britain was stuck with another set of colonies that it had to staff with officials and defend with troops.

Planting the Flag

While Great Britain and other European countries scrambled for colonies, the actual taking of power took on an almost comical aspect. This 1884 photograph in *The Cambridge Illustrated History of the British Empire*, edited by P. J. Marshall, shows the Union Jack being raised over a small frame building in Papua New Guinea. As rows of British sailors and marines are lined up smartly, a group of almost naked natives stare curiously.

Fifty native chiefs had been summoned to the ceremony. They were given presents of butcher knives, cloth, tobacco, and small statues of Queen Victoria. The queen, they were told, "now guards and watches over you, looks upon you as her children."

When the Germans began grabbing South Pacific islands, their assumption of power was even more informal. In 1886 a gunboat cruised the Solomon Islands. At each island a landing party went ashore and gave the local chiefs gifts and an elaborate proclamation. The sailors put up a sign reading "German Imperial Protectorate," the German flag was raised and lowered, and then the Germans rowed back to their ship, which proceeded to the next island and repeated the process.

Uganda

The Germans influenced the British to take Uganda in much the same way that the French had burdened them with the Sudan. Carl Peters, a German explorer who had been instrumental in the takeover of Tanganyika, planned to do the same thing in Uganda. Since the headwaters of the Nile River lay in the area, Egypt was threatened. In 1890 Britain and Germany reached an agreement: Uganda would go to the British in exchange for Britain's recognition of Germany's claim in Tanganyika.

The British even sweetened the pot by ceding the tiny North Sea island of Helgoland to the Germans, an action with which Queen Victoria did not agree. "Giving up what one had is always a bad thing,"[12] she cautioned Prime Minister Benjamin Disraeli.

The African pattern was repeated in the South Pacific. Britain had been content to have informal control, through the presence of the Royal Navy, in the vast area north of Australia. In the 1880s, however, France and Germany began staking claims to various islands, including strategically important New Guinea. Although this part of the world was not nearly as important to Britain as Africa was, the British hastened to conclude a series of agreements. Britain got the Papua section of New Guinea, the Gilbert Islands, and part of the Solomon Islands.

In the short term, German expansion in the late 1800s propelled Britain into the governorship of a multitude of possessions that it could not afford but that it thought it could not afford anyone else to have. The long-term results were much more serious: The colonial rivalry between the two nations was an underlying cause of World War I.

Russia

Russia, like Germany, was a late entry into the race for colonies. Russia's economy was not as strong as that of Germany, but it had much more in terms of population and natural resources. But what made Great Britain most wary of Russia was that, of all the European powers, it was closest to India.

For centuries, Russia's dream had been to have a warm-water port, one that could be used year-round. The obvious choice was Constantinople (modern-day Istanbul), the capital of Turkey. Britain, to ensure naval supremacy in the Mediterranean, had to keep Constantinople in the hands of the weak Turks rather than an increasingly strong Russia.

British Highlanders lead an assault on the Russians during the Crimean War.

Turkey had managed to keep Russia away from Constantinople in 1828, but the Russians tried again in 1853. This time, Britain intervened. The result was the Crimean War of 1854–1856, the only colonial war ever fought between Britain and another European power.

The Russians were defeated, but in 1877 they marched south once more. This time, the British, by threatening to go to war, forced the Russians to sign a peace treaty that guaranteed that Constantinople would remain in Turkish hands.

Unlike Britain's confrontations with France and Germany in Africa, the conflict with Russia over Constantinople led to no new British colonies. However, it was extremely costly, because, over the course of fifty years, the British poured money into Turkey to help it withstand its larger, aggressive neighbor.

The Afghan Wars

The other threat from Russia was not to a route to India but to India itself. Between the two countries lay Afghanistan. The area of India bordered by Afghanistan was the Northwest Frontier, its most vulnerable.

Trouble Everywhere

For most of the 1800s Great Britain was unrivaled on the world scene. After 1870, however, it seemed as if competitors were springing up everywhere. As soon as one confrontation was settled, another one began. Soon, the British were beleaguered on all sides. In 1885, the *Pall Mall Gazette* (as quoted in *The Lion's Share* by Bernard Porter) complained,

> We have avoided trouble hitherto by knuckling down humbly all around the world. We have brought all this trouble in Egypt on our heads out of the desire to oblige France . . . and still our neighbors are not satisfied. Prince Bismarck (of Germany) orders us out of the north-eastern corner of New Guinea, and we take up our hat and go. France tears up our own financial proposals, and we humbly accept her alternative scheme. . . . With the cream of our available fighting force locked up in the Soudan, what can we do but give in here, give in there, and give in everywhere all round the world until at last we are sharply brought up by some demand to which we cannot give in—and then! How are we prepared for that eventuality, which will come as certain as the summer sun?

In 1874, Britain decided that Afghanistan was too vulnerable to Russian attack. The British demanded that the Afghan ruler admit British "advisers" to his capital, Kabul, but he refused. The viceroy of India, Lord Lytton, tried to force the issue by sending in an armed force in 1878, but it was defeated.

Britain did not want war with Afghanistan. Disraeli was furious at Lytton's blunder, but the "insult" to Britain had to be avenged and its prestige reasserted. Accordingly, war was declared on Afghanistan, and in 1879 it became a British protectorate. As with so many other parts of the British empire, Afghanistan contributed no wealth, only a measure of security for India, and cost the British dearly.

The other area where Britain feared Russian expansion was in the Far East. As with Constantinople, the Russians wanted a warm-water port in the Pacific, and they had their eyes on Korea. Britain did not consider Japan a potential rival and did not want to see Russia increase its power in the Pacific. The British helped Japan build its navy, which scored a decisive victory over Russia in 1904. The British had also entered into an alliance with Japan in 1902 that had enabled it to take on Russia without fear of intervention from any other European power.

Japan

The alliance with Japan in 1902 must have seemed like a good idea to the British at the time. Twenty years later they were having second thoughts. The Japanese aided the British during World War I but seized several German islands in the process. After the war, they embarked on a program of militarism and expansion.

Japan's emergence as a major power in the Pacific alarmed both Britain and the United States. In 1922 they sought to restrict the Japanese navy through a treaty limiting its battleship fleet to 60 percent of those of the other two nations.

Japan, however, could concentrate its navy in the Pacific, whereas Britain's was spread worldwide. Britain thought it needed a major military stronghold—a Pacific version of Gibraltar—and chose Singapore. During the 1920s and 1930s, a huge naval base was constructed with port facilities for the mighty ships and massive concrete bunkers bristling with guns capable of hitting targets more than fifty miles away.

The cost was enormous—about £60 million—and came during a time when the British economy had been severely strained by World War I and a postwar depression. The supposedly invulnerable "Fortress Singapore" was the single largest British expenditure between the world wars.

As things turned out, that expenditure was for nothing. When the Japanese attacked in 1941, the battleships were sunk by aircraft and the Japanese army moved swiftly through presumably impenetrable jungle north of the city. Singapore surrendered on February 15, 1942, and more than 100,000 British soldiers, most of whom had not fired a shot, spent the rest of the war in prison camps.

The United States

The United States, once a colony itself, has historically shown an aversion to colonial empires. Although it has had possessions, the larger ones such as the Philippines, Hawaii, and Alaska have either become states or achieved independence. The United States has done everything possible to prevent other powers from obtaining colonies in the Western Hemisphere and has done nothing to help those powers gain colonies elsewhere.

In the Monroe Doctrine of 1823, the United States, while recognizing existing European colonies in the Americas, vowed to oppose any further colonization. Although the United States lacked the military power to withstand Britain had Britain wanted more American colonies, the British were content to expand elsewhere and, at first, left the Americas alone. Only once, in 1848, did Britain consider creating a presence in Oregon. After a stern warning from President James K. Polk, it backed off.

By World War II, however, the military position was completely reversed. The United States was far more powerful and thus able to dictate the course of the war. It made very plain to the British, in the words of *Life* magazine, that "One thing we are sure we are not fighting for is to hold the British Empire together."[13] As a result, President Franklin Roosevelt and his military leaders vetoed campaigns such as the invasion through Greece proposed by British prime minister Winston Churchill because they thought his primary goal was to protect British interests in the Middle East.

American leaders draft the Monroe Doctrine in 1823. The doctrine declared America's policy against further colonization in the Americas.

Livingstone's Legacy

Before the rapid increase of European imperialism in the second half of the 1800s, African colonies were scattered along the coast. Knowledge of the interior was slight, but much of that knowledge would be furnished by one remarkable man, Dr. David Livingstone.

A Scottish missionary, explorer, and doctor, Livingstone arrived in South Africa in 1840 and for more than thirty years spent most of his life going where no Europeans had ever been. He brought medical care and Christianity to the tribes he encountered, and his reports back to the Royal Geographical Society raised public and governmental awareness of opportunities in Africa.

Scottish missionary and explorer Dr. David Livingstone became famous for his extensive travels throughout Africa.

Livingstone became famous in Britain. Newspapers and journals regularly carried articles about his explorations and adventures. Livingstone generated great concern in 1869 when he had not been heard from since setting out to find the source of the Nile River three years earlier. An American newspaper, the *New York Herald,* commissioned another British explorer, Henry Stanley, to find Livingstone.

After almost two years of searching, Stanley was successful. He reached the village of Ujiji on Lake Tanganyika, found the missionary ill and short of supplies, and greeted him with the famous words, "Dr. Livingstone, I presume."

Stanley tried to persuade Livingstone to return with him, but he was unsuccessful. Livingstone died two years later and is buried in Westminster Abbey in London. His explorations paved the way for the colonization of Central Africa, but his influence contributed to the end of the British Empire, and all European rule, in Africa. He firmly believed that Africans could be self-governing and develop modern nations. By constantly emphasizing the Africans' potential to them, he may well have set the stage for African nationalism in the next century.

Also, the British were informed that the United States believed that people should determine their own political fate and that this applied to British colonies such as India, where an independence movement gained momentum after the war. Since Britain was now so economically dependent on the United States, it had no choice but to begin letting the pieces of the empire go their own way. "The Americans have got us by the short hairs," said a British official in India. "We can't do anything in this theatre [region], amphibious or otherwise, without material assistance from them. So if they don't approve they don't provide."[14] This stance by the United States was the single most important cause of the rapid disintegration of the British Empire after World War II.

An important factor in Britain's dealings with rival powers was that it needed to deal with them one at a time. Some of the confrontations occurred simultaneously, and the British had to walk a fine line to avoid becoming too involved on too many fronts. The acquisition of Tanganyika by Germany, for instance, was not strenuously opposed because the British were tied up in Egypt at the same time.

The net effect of the spread of European imperialism in the late 1800s was that it forced Great Britain to expand the empire more than was wanted, more than was necessary, and more than was sensible. Lord George Hamilton, secretary for India, summed up the situation when he wrote in 1899, "I think all my colleagues feel as I do that . . . our Empire is in excess of our armaments, or even of our power to defend it in all parts of the world."[15]

Victory's Bitter Fruits

A RMED CONFLICT PLAYED a major role in the rise of the British Empire. Oddly enough, it played just as great a part in its decline. Even though none of the major wars were lost, the victories carried within them the seeds of destruction of that which they were fought to gain and protect.

After the victory over France and Napoleon Bonaparte in 1815, Britain went without a major war till almost the end of the century, except for the Crimean War against Russia in the 1850s. The next half-century, however, saw Britain in three protracted struggles: the Boer War (1899–1902), World War I (1914–1918), and World War II (1939–1945). The British were ultimately victorious in all three, but they drained the nation of both manpower and money, damaged British prestige at home and throughout the world, and resulted in some promises that proved difficult to keep.

The Boer War

In 1877, Britain annexed the Orange Free State and the Transvaal, the two Boer republics of southern Africa. When they rebelled in 1881 and defeated a British army at Majuba, Prime Minister Gladstone, whose hands were full elsewhere, agreed to restore their independence, provided that Britain could retain some vague control over foreign policy. To Britain, the Boer republics were not worth the trouble of conquering them.

They became worth the trouble in 1886 when huge deposits of gold were discovered in the Witwatersrand area of the Transvaal. The Transvaal now was more valuable than the Cape Colony, and

35

A Shameful Legacy

Although most people associate them with Nazi Germany, it was the British who invented one of the most terrible aspects of twentieth-century warfare—the concentration camp—during the Boer War of 1899–1902. It was one of the least glorious times in the history of the British Empire and one that left a legacy of outrage worldwide.

When the South African Boers adopted hit-and-run guerrilla warfare in 1900, the British responded with a scorched earth policy, burning Boer farms, killing livestock, destroying crops, and imprisoning thousands of men, women, and children. Conditions in the camps were horrible, and more than nineteen thousand civilians died in them over a two-year period.

These conditions were brought to light and publicized by Emily Hobhouse, an energetic reformer from England who was repeatedly arrested and expelled from South Africa by British authorities. These are her observations, as quoted in *The Boer War* by Thomas Pakenham:

> The shelter was totally insufficient. When the 8, 10, or 12 persons who occupied a bell-tent were all packed into it, either to escape from the fierceness of the sun or dust or rain storms, there was no room to move, and the atmosphere was indescribable, even with the duly lifted flaps. There was no soap provided. The water supplied would not go round. . . . The ration . . . was sufficiently small, but when . . . the actual amount did not come up to the scale, it became a starvation rate. . . . No wonder sickness abounds. Since I left here six weeks ago there have been 62 deaths in camp, and the doctor himself is down with enteric [typhoid fever]. Two of the Boer girls we had trained as nurses and who were doing good work are dead, too.

Britain—namely millionaire miner Cecil Rhodes—wanted it. Rhodes began to build a case for war with the government in London, arguing that the Germans might take over the Boer republics instead and link up with their colony of South-West Africa to block the missionary route to the British territories to the north.

Rhodes tried to force the issue. On his orders, troops led by Leander Jameson invaded the Transvaal in 1895, supposedly to safeguard the Uitlanders (Outlanders), mostly British miners who had flocked to hunt for gold, who were rebelling against Boer rule. The only trouble was that no rebellion had taken place. Jameson was easily defeated, and Britain was made to look foolish in the eyes of the world. The episode also convinced the Boer leader, Paul Kruger, that the British might be beaten.

Britain, in the mid-1890s, was tired of colonial conflicts, and the government knew it. A war with the Boers, Joseph Chamberlain, secretary of state for the colonies, said in 1897, "would be in the nature of a Civil War, a long war, a bitter war, a costly war." [16] Nevertheless, he was convinced that war was necessary and set out to sway British public opinion. As he told young Winston Churchill, "It's no use blowing the trumpet for the charge and then looking around to find nobody following." [17]

The Propaganda Battle

The German scare was emphasized by the press. The Boers were pictured by ministers as barbarians who cruelly mistreated the African natives. Finally, aided by a Boer ultimatum in 1899, war was declared, with the Orange Free State joining the Transvaal.

The Boer War was a disaster for Britain from the very beginning. British troops found themselves fighting not natives with spears but a determined enemy with modern weapons. The Boers quickly besieged key cities, which were relieved only after massive British reinforcements were sent and after fierce fighting.

Boer soldiers line the trenches during the Boer War in 1899.

In 1900, however, the British prevailed, outflanking the Boer armies with swift cavalry movements. But when it appeared that the end of the war was near, the Boers changed tactics. They abandoned massed formations and used what later would be called guerrilla warfare, striking camps and communication lines.

The British retaliated much as American forces would decades later in Vietnam, burning Boer farms and villages, killing livestock, and rounding up and detaining everyone—men, women, and children. Finally, the brutal methods paid off and the Boers accepted a treaty in 1902 that made them part of the British Empire.

The Vulnerable Giant

The British had won the Boer War, but they had suffered dramatic and permanent damage to their reputation. To begin with, the myth of British invincibility on the battlefield was smashed. The British public, as well as the rest of the world, watched—amazed—as the vaunted British army was fought to a standstill by what most regarded as a gaggle of farmers. Not only Britain's European rivals but also its subject populations in colonies around the world realized how vulnerable the British lion was.

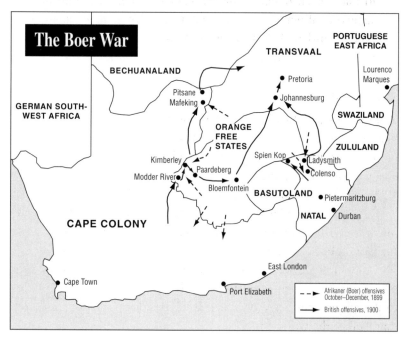

The war also dampened imperialistic fervor in Britain itself. The British had entered the war full of "patriotic fever," a phrase one recruit wrote down as his reason for enlisting. The long casualty lists—more than twenty thousand dead—and the enormous cost—£450 million—made the British wonder if it was worthwhile, especially when the underlying cause seemed to be greed rather than glory.

More than anything, however, the British treatment of both prisoners of war and civilians outraged public opinion, at home and around the world. The British Empire had grown, in part, on the moral principle of bringing civilized behavior to far-flung reaches of the world. Morality was hard to argue in the face of thousands of women and children dying in captivity because of unsanitary conditions.

The Boer War marked the real beginning of the downfall of the British Empire. There had been a few outward signs, but those signs now were visible to everyone. As historian Bernard Porter wrote,

> By the time it [the war] was won . . . it seemed to many that it had exhausted the imperial enthusiasm of the people, and even of the government. In the years it had left to it the [Conservative Party] government was careful not to repeat it, not to make such demands on the people again. . . . With the Japanese alliance of 1902 and then with a new entente [agreement] with France in 1904, it tacitly abandoned the pretence that Britain could go it alone any more.[18]

World War I

The race for colonies in the late 1800s eventually reached the point where there were no unclaimed lands left for European nations to grab. The nations' only option was to vie for one another's colonies. The tensions among the imperial powers increased during the early 1900s and erupted in 1914 in what was known then as the Great War.

It was not called a world war at the time, and most of the fighting was confined to Europe. But it was a world war in a real sense for Britain because it was fought to preserve the British Empire.

As with the Boer War, Britain emerged victorious, but only after a long, deadly, expensive struggle. The victory added vast territories to the empire but actually left it weaker and under stronger attack than before the war.

The British military had been weakened by thirty years of conflicts over its vast holdings. Germany was the strongest enemy it had faced since Napoleon, and the first two years of the war resulted in a bloody deadlock. Britain needed all the help it could get, from wherever it could find it, and to get that help the British began to make promises.

Britain needed troops from India, not only British troops but native troops as well. In order to be able to send troops from India to France, the British needed peace in India. Mohandas Gandhi, a British-educated attorney and leader of the Indian National Congress dedicated to self-rule for Indians, recognized the opportunity, saying, "The gateway to our freedom is situated on French soil."[19]

In 1916, Edwin Montagu, secretary of state for India, declared Britain's intent to foster "the gradual development of self-governing institutions"[20] in India. Things didn't work out that way. Even though sixty-five thousand Indians died fighting for Great Britain, India found itself little closer to freedom. The Indians now knew Britain could not be trusted to keep its promises, and the next twenty years saw a rapid increase in agitation that eventually led to the loss of India.

More than a million Indian troops, such as these officers standing with the Union Jack flag, fought for Britain during World War I.

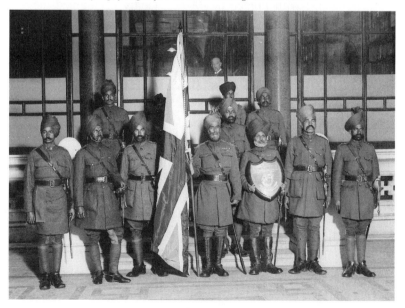

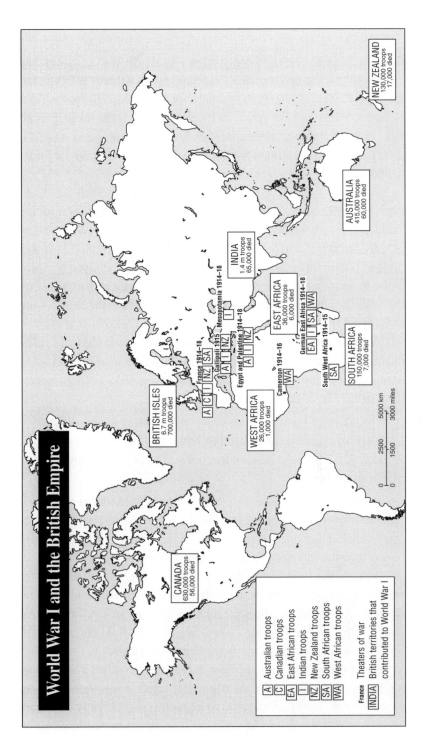

World War I and the British Empire

CANADA
630,000 troops
56,000 died

BRITISH ISLES
6.7 m troops
700,000 died

France 1914–18
A C I NZ SA

Gallipoli 1915
A I NZ

Egypt and Palestine 1914–18
A I NZ

Mesopotamia 1914–18
I

WEST AFRICA
26,000 troops
1,000 died

Cameroon 1914–16
WA

INDIA
1.4 m troops
65,000 died

EAST AFRICA
36,000 troops
6,000 died

German East Africa 1914–18
EA I SA WA

South West Africa 1914–15
SA

SOUTH AFRICA
150,000 troops
7,000 died

AUSTRALIA
415,000 troops
60,000 died

NEW ZEALAND
130,000 troops
17,000 died

0   2500   5000 km
0   1500   3000 miles

A   Australian troops
C   Canadian troops
EA   East African troops
I   Indian troops
NZ   New Zealand troops
SA   South African troops
WA   West African troops

France   Theaters of war
INDIA   British territories that
         contributed to World War I

Promises

Germany was not Britain's only enemy in World War I. Turkey had come into the war on Germany's side and posed a threat to Egypt and the Suez Canal. Again, Britain could not divert enough troops from France to withstand the Turks, so it turned to the Arabs for help as allies. In 1915 the high commissioner for Egypt, Sir Henry MacMahon, promised that Britain would "recognize and support the independence of the Arabs"[21] in exchange for their help.

With the help of British intelligence officers such as T. E. Lawrence ("Lawrence of Arabia"), the Arabs revolted against the Turks and greatly helped the British cause. After the war, however, no independence was forthcoming. Instead, most of the Middle East was divided between Britain and France. The Arabs felt betrayed and, just as the Indians, began an active independence movement. By stirring up the Arabs against the Turks, said one British politician, the British were creating "a Frankenstein's monster"[22] that would turn on its maker.

An even more troublesome promise in the Middle East was made to the Jews, who had been settling in Palestine in ever-increasing numbers since the last decade of the 1800s. In 1917 Foreign Secretary Arthur James Balfour wrote,

> His Majesty's government views with favour the establishment in Palestine of a national home for the Jewish people and will use their best endeavors to facilitate the achievement of this object.[23]

Britain did not need the help of the Jews in Palestine as much as it did the support of influential Jews in the United States, which had recently come into the war. Also, they foresaw "a prosperous community bound to Britain by ties of gratitude and interest"[24] after the war.

As were the Indians and the Arabs, the Jews of Palestine were severely disappointed after the war when Britain, fearful of the reaction of the Arabs, failed to follow through on the Balfour Declaration. An underground war against the British began and would continue until World War II, damaging British prestige worldwide.

Great Britain was damaged not only by the promises it made during World War I but also by the war itself. The cost was tremendous in terms of both money and lives. The economy was severely damaged. More than 700,000 Britons were killed. The survivors, disillusioned by

Lawrence of Arabia

During World War I, with the British military stretched to the limit, intelligence officers worked with Arab leaders, helping them to rebel against Turkey, an ally of Germany. By far the most famous and flamboyant of the "Arabists" was Colonel T. E. Lawrence, known to history as "Lawrence of Arabia."

Wearing Arab dress, learning their customs and language, and leading them into battle, Lawrence became a hero to the Arabs and a major thorn in the side of the Turks. He was wounded several times and on one occasion was captured and tortured before escaping.

As did the other British officers, Lawrence tempted the Arabs with promises of freedom, even though he knew that the Sykes-Picot Agreement, signed in 1916, divided the Middle East between Britain and France. "I risked the fraud," he said (quoted in *The Lion's Share* by Bernard Porter), "on the conviction that Arab help was necessary to our cheap and speedy victory in the East, and that better we win and break our word than lose."

He was not proud of what he had done. In *The Cambridge History of the British Empire,* he is quoted as having said that the Arabs "did not risk their lives in battle to change masters, to become British subjects or French citizens, but to win a show of their own."

Legendary British colonel T. E. Lawrence joined forces with the Arabs to rebel against Turkey.

Lawrence was so disillusioned that, when offered a medal by King George V at a palace ceremony, he politely declined, leaving the stunned monarch with the box in his hand. He retired from the army and had some success as an author, including *The Seven Pillars of Wisdom* about his experiences in Arabia. He died in 1935, at age forty-six, of injuries sustained in a motorcycle accident.

the long conflict, had a different view of the world than they had before the war. The war not only killed soldiers but also destroyed Britain's enthusiasm for empire building.

Another 200,000 soldiers from throughout the empire were killed, including 56,000 from Canada and 60,000 from Australia. The older, settled parts of the empire had given much to support the mother country and would demand an ever-greater independence. Indeed, between the world wars, the dominions—Canada, New Zealand, Australia, and South Africa—became part of the British Empire not even in name but as part of the British "Commonwealth."

World War II

The outbreak of World War II in 1939 saw the British Empire larger than it ever had been or would be. That was the problem. The empire had grown so huge that it proved impossible to defend. It had barely held up in World War I facing one major enemy. In 1940, facing two potent opponents—Germany and Japan—it cracked.

Only two months after the Japanese entered the war they captured Singapore, Britain's stronghold in the Far East. Prime Minister Winston Churchill called it "the greatest disaster to British arms our history records."[25] The damage, however, went far beyond military losses. The

Japanese tanks roll through Singapore at the start of World War II. The Japanese attack on Britain's stronghold in the Far East shattered the myth of Anglo superiority.

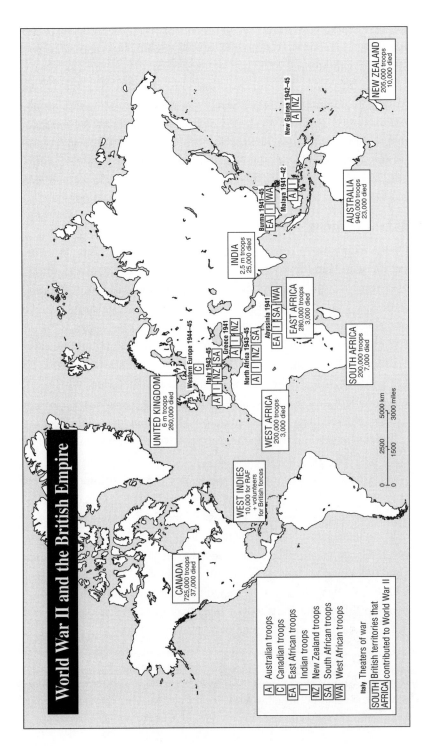

World War II and the British Empire

NEW ZEALAND
205,000 troops
10,000 died

New Guinea 1942-45
| A | NZ |

AUSTRALIA
940,000 troops
23,000 died

Burma 1941-45
| EA | I | WA |

Malaya 1941-42
| A | I |

INDIA
2.5 m troops
25,000 died

EAST AFRICA
280,000 troops
3,000 died

Abyssinia 1941
| EA | I | SA | WA |

SOUTH AFRICA
200,000 troops
7,000 died

Greece 1941
| A | I | NZ |

North Africa 1943-45
| A | I | NZ | SA |

Italy 1943-45
| A | I | NZ | SA |

Western Europe 1944-45
| C |

UNITED KINGDOM
6 m troops
260,000 died

WEST AFRICA
200,000 troops
3,000 died

WEST INDIES
10,000 for RAF
+ volunteers
for British forces

0   2500   5000 km
0   1500   3000 miles

CANADA
725,000 troops
37,000 died

| A | Australian troops
| C | Canadian troops
| EA | East African troops
| I | Indian troops
| NZ | New Zealand troops
| SA | South African troops
| WA | West African troops

Italy Theaters of war

| SOUTH AFRICA | British territories that contributed to World War II

world's greatest power had been defeated, not by a rival European power but by a "colored" opponent. The mystique of Anglo superiority was shattered, and millions of nonwhites throughout the empire took notice.

The difference was apparent in India. Shortly after the fall of Singapore, Churchill sent Sir Stanford Cripps to India with a proposition for Gandhi and Jawaharlal Nehru, the leaders of the independence movement. In exchange for support during the war, Britain promised something just short of full independence after the conflict ended. Full independence, however, was just what India wanted, and it now felt in a strong enough position to refuse the offer.

A New Outlook

On the whole, however, the nonwhite colonies supported Britain during the war. Had they not, the outcome might have been very different. Some 2.5 million Indians fought for the Allies, as did 680,000 Africans. But although they helped win the war, their aid had its price. Their eyes had been opened to their opportunities for freedom and the power they had to achieve it. As one British politician said,

> We shall see after the war a very large number of [nonwhites] going home . . . with a sense of discipline, with a knowledge of English, and educated in a broad sense, by travel. Now they will be going home, in some places, to distant villages and remote districts, and to the old life, but seeing it with very different eyes.[26]

The other principal impact of World War II was that, although it had entered the war the world's strongest power, Britain emerged no better than a poor third to the United States and the Soviet Union. Britain had held the line against Nazi Germany by itself from May 1940 to December 1941; the effort had not only depleted its military strength but had also bankrupted the country. The national debt in 1945 was a staggering £30 billion, most of it owed to the United States. The postwar economic boom that sent Americans to new heights of prosperity never happened in Britain, and the empire became even more of a luxury.

Aversion to Empire

Both the Americans and Soviets were opposed to empires on principle. The British could deal with Soviet opposition. The alliance had been one of convenience, never one of friendship. The Americans were another matter. In 1941, President Franklin Roosevelt warned, "There must be no place after the war for special privileges, either for individuals or for nations."[27]

In 1941, desperate for American help, Churchill had agreed to the Atlantic Charter, a statement endorsing the right of people everywhere to choose their forms of government. Britain had made promises before, but this one was harder to get around. Double-dealing with Indians and Arabs was one thing; deceiving a partner more powerful than you and to whom you owed billions of dollars was another. After the war, when the United States made it clear that Britain was expected to live up to the agreement, the empire quickly began to crumble.

The Boer War, World War I, and World War II—the British had won all three but had lost their world supremacy in the process. In fighting to preserve the British Empire, they had lost it. It had simply become too big and too expensive. As Prime Minister William Gladstone had said as far back as 1900, "You must divide victories by taxation if you wish to know in solid figures the real worth of Empire."[28]

The Cost of
Chapter 4 Conquest

THE BRITISH PREFERRED TO talk and write about loftier aims—the spread of civilization and the conversion of the heathen to Christianity—but the underlying motive for the creation, growth, and maintenance of their empire was profit. A pamphlet in 1620 boasted that the new Massachusetts Bay Colony in America would provide the mother country with "the Wines, Fruit and Salt of France and Spain" and "the silks of Persia and Italy."[29] And economist William Jevons boasted in 1865 that Britain was the economic center of the universe:

> The plains of North America are our corn fields; Chicago and Odessa our granaries; Canada and the Baltic are our timber forests; Australasia contains our sheep farms, and in Argentina and on the western prairies of North America are our herds of oxen; Peru sends her silver, and the gold of south Africa and Australia flows to London; the Hindus and the Chinese grow tea for us, and our coffee, sugar and spice plantations are in all the Indies.[30]

As the empire grew rapidly in the late 1800s, one critic, John Morley, complained, "All this Empire-building! Why, the whole thing is tainted with the spirit of the hunt for gold."[31] The British public saw nothing particularly wrong with this view. As late as 1924, Edward, Prince of Wales, called on his nation to "work unitedly and energetically to develop the resources of the Empire for the benefit of the British race."[32]

Quest for Growth

The way to more profit, most of Britain reasoned, was more colonies. Surely, bigger was better. A patriotic fervor swept the nation as the

48

Union Jack was raised above more and more territory, and the empire, in the words of the song "Land of Hope and Glory," grew "wider still and wider."

Not everyone was convinced. Prime Minister William Gladstone once complained to empire builder Cecil Rhodes, "Our burden is too great. We have too much, Mr. Rhodes, to do. Apart from increasing our obligations in every part of the world, what advantage do you see to the English race in acquisition of new territory?"[33] And Rudyard Kipling, in his 1897 poem *Recessional*, warned against becoming "drunk with sight of power" and foresaw a time when

> The tumult and the shouting dies;
> The Captains and the Kings depart.[34]

Gladstone and Kipling proved to be correct. The British Empire grew so large and so complex that the cost of maintaining and protecting it became greater than the benefits it brought. When this became evident in the period between the world wars, the end of the empire was inevitable.

British prime minister William Gladstone recognized early on that maintaining and protecting the British colonies had become unmanageable.

Mercantilism

In its early stages, the British Empire was a mercantile system. That is, the colonies were tightly bound economically to the mother country. Laws such as the Navigation Acts and the Stamp Act ensured that most trade would be conducted with Britain, in British ships, and on British terms. Such measures were a prime cause of the American War of Independence.

Starting about 1820 the economic wind shifted. The mercantile system had been based on the belief that a country's wealth and resources were finite and had to be protected from rivals. However, economist Adam Smith, in his 1776 classic *The Wealth of Nations*, argued that wealth could expand indefinitely if trade was not restricted. His theories were borne out after the American Revolution; Britain's trade with its former colony almost doubled in the twenty years after American independence was won.

From 1820 until 1870, then, Britain prospered greatly under the principles of free trade. It was easy to see why. It had an overwhelming superiority in merchant ships and, thanks to its remaining colonies, a healthy flow of natural resources to fuel a rapidly expanding manufacturing base. Even when free to trade with any country, most countries found that Britain furnished superior goods at the best prices.

The Informal Empire

During this period, few colonies were added. There was no need. Thanks to its economic superiority, Britain built up an "informal" empire. British companies were powerful in countries such as Argentina, China, and Egypt, and they exercised considerable political influence. As one British politician put it, "Foreign nations would become valuable Colonies to us, without imposing on us the responsibility of governing them."[35] This informal empire was so successful that in the 1850s some free traders proposed cutting political links with the colonies altogether.

The free trade boom lasted only as long as Britain had no serious commercial rivals. Such rivals began to emerge in the 1870s as Germany and the United States started gaining a greater share of world trade. Both nations surpassed Britain in steel production. And more

A Rebellious Daughter

The most independent-minded of the British colonies when it came to economics was Canada. Even though Great Britain was committed to free trade, the Canadians took action to protect their native industries by placing a tariff, or tax, on foreign goods, even including those from Britain, as early as the 1860s. The Canadians also took exception to having to pay the cost of British troops in Canada.

In the face of such independence, the *Times* of London huffed (as quoted in *The Cambridge Illustrated History of the British Empire*),

> Opinion in England is perfectly decided that in the connexion between the Mother Country and the Colony the advantage is infinitely more on the side of the child than of the parent. . . . We cannot even obtain reasonably fair treatment for our own manufactures, which are taxed 25 per cent on their value to increase a revenue which the colonies will not apply to our or even to their defence. There is little reciprocity in such a relation.

Canada's attitude was summed up in a poem by Rudyard Kipling:

> A Nation spoke to a Nation,
> A Throne send word to a Throne,
> Daughter am I in my mother's house,
> But mistress in my own.

---

countries—including some British colonies—began to buy American textiles rather than British. In the 1890s British exports declined for the first time in living memory. The problem was compounded by British investors who found they could make more money investing in foreign countries than in British colonies.

The new international rivalries were more than economic. Germany and France began expanding their colonial empires, forcing Britain to do likewise. New territories were snapped up, first in Africa and the Pacific and later in the Middle East. In areas such as Egypt, formal control replaced the old informal empire. Conquering these new areas cost money, as did setting up the governments to run them.

Unproductive Colonies

It had been traditional British policy that the colonies would be self-supporting, that the cost of governing and guarding them would be

The Big Hole

Diamond miners in Kimberley, South Africa, stand in what was to become the largest excavated site in the world.

The lure of wealth in the British colonies was strongest in South Africa, with its gold and diamond mines. The best example of the frenzy created by the discovery of a new source of riches was the Big Hole at Kimberley.

Within weeks of the first strike in the 1890s, the area was swarming with prospectors, each of whom had laid claim to a small plot of land. As the pits grew deeper, the narrow roads between them collapsed, and the area finally was one huge excavation. The only way to get diamond ore out of the pit was with a rope and bucket. Each miner had his own rope, and the pit was soon covered in a tangled mesh of lines.

The Big Hole was eventually bought in its entirety by Cecil Rhodes for more than £5 million. By the time the mine played out in 1914, the hole was a mile in diameter and almost seven hundred feet deep—the largest man-made hole in the world.

borne by the colonists. That was fine as long as the colony had a viable economy such as that of India or Canada. The trouble was that, in many of the newer territories, trade did not "follow the flag." In 1897, the entire vast area of tropical Africa accounted for only 1.2 percent of British trade.

Britain was still far and away the world's most powerful nation and its overseas empire still was a source of great wealth, but critics were beginning to ask exactly where this wealth was going and to whom. In 1902, economist J. A. Hobson published *Imperialism: A Study*, in which he suggested that the economic benefits of the empire went to capitalists and investors and not to Britain as a whole. The British people, he argued, would be much better off if the money spent on armies in Afghanistan were spent on hospitals in Hampshire instead.

An increasing number of people in Britain were starting to have thoughts similar to Hobson's. The Labour Party, founded in 1906, was interested much more in the welfare of the ordinary Briton than in foreign conquests, and the feeling grew after the Boer War, which not only had burst the bubble of British invincibility but had also been a huge drain on the economy. The military commander, Lord

With self-supporting industries such as tea plantations, India, unlike many other British territories, was an economically viable colony.

Kitchener, admitted that his forces were incapable of meeting their worldwide commitments: "We are in the position of a firm which has written cheques against a non-existent balance." [36]

Economic Troubles

Britain's national pride never fully recovered from the Boer War. The economy did, but just in time to be hit with another disaster—World War I. In addition to costing the British 700,000 lives, it had cost virtually the entire treasury. Overseas investments had to be sold off to pay the war debt. After the war, industry was stagnant and unemployment high.

The British people were in no mood to spend money, particularly on the military—even on the navy that had been the bulwark of the empire. Britain had always maintained a "two power" standard; that is, the Royal Navy should be larger than the two largest foreign navies combined. In 1922, however, the British gave in to political and economic reality, agreeing to a treaty that put their navy at the same level as that of the United States.

A Royal Navy battle cruiser in port after World War I. Until 1922, Britain took pride in claiming the largest navy in the world.

The economy continued to decline. Britain's share of world trade, which had been 25 percent in 1860, fell to 14 percent by 1938. Overseas investments fell £1 billion from 1914 to 1930. The only area in which trade increased was with the various members of the empire. So to protect the markets left to them, the British abandoned free trade after more than a century. At the Ottawa (Canada) Conference of 1932, protective tariffs were reintroduced. Britain felt that it had no choice. It was no longer strong enough or rich enough to dictate to the rest of the world. As Colonial Secretary Leopold Amery said, Britain needed

> an imperial economic policy based on the mutual development of our common resources of nature and human skill, and on the maintenance of a standard of living which we set for ourselves, and are not simply content to have set for us by the unlimited and unregulated competition of the world outside.[37]

The Dominions

The empire, however, especially the largely self-governing dominions of Canada, Australia, New Zealand, and South Africa, was less than enthusiastic. They had sent thousands of their sons to die for Great Britain and now demanded more, not less, freedom of trade. Despite the measures taken by Britain, the dominions refused to sacrifice their own well-being for that of the British. Their trade outside the empire, especially with the United States, continued to increase. Thus, even though Britain's trade with the empire was the healthiest part of its economy, it was nowhere near what it had been.

Economic weakness translated into diplomatic hesitancy. The British, once ready to fight anyone, anywhere, now shied away from conflict. When the Japanese attacked China in 1937, Britain remained silent. "No good blustering," said Sir Alexander Cadogan, "unless we are sure we can carry out our threats."[38] Since Britain could not afford a war, it did everything it could to prevent one, including appeasing German dictator Adolf Hitler. The result was World War II.

World War II left Britain victorious but almost bankrupt. Foreign investments had been sold off to finance the fight for survival. The country's infrastructure—everything from factory machinery to the electrical systems—was in a shambles. Basic necessities such as food and gasoline remained strictly rationed. The British public

Room to Grow

One of the empire's greatest economic benefits to Great Britain was that it served as an outlet for emigration. The population of Britain swelled in the mid-1800s, fueled by the industrial revolution. Emigration to the colonies was one way in which severe unemployment was avoided. One emigrant, James Dobbie, found life in Lanark, Canada, far more rewarding than in England. He urged his father to join him in Canada in this 1826 letter, found in *The Rise and Fall of the British Empire* by Lawrence James:

> I really bless God every day I rise, that He was ever pleased in the course of his providence to send me and my family to this place. We are not without difficulties here, but they are nothing to your wants in Glasgow [Scotland]; we have always plenty to eat and drink, and have always a little to spare. . . . I wish you would try and do all you can to come out: you will find plenty of work, and hard work, but be assured it will pay well. My stock of cattle consists of one yoke of oxen, three milk cows and three young ones. I have got up a very handsome house, with the assistance of fifteen young men it was raised in one day; it is 24 feet in length and 15 in breadth.

wanted nothing more to do with the empire. They were weary of talk of glory and only wanted their country rebuilt. The empire, once viewed with pride, had now become a burden.

The Labour Government

The mood of weariness showed up even before the end of the war: In early 1945, the British turned their backs on Winston Churchill and the Conservative Party and elected the first Labour Party government in the country's history. The new prime minister, Clement Atlee, had a much clearer vision of the world's new realities than had Churchill, whose outlook was rooted in the previous century. Atlee saw that the days of empire were numbered and that it could survive only in a form in which territories were self-supporting, self-governing, and equal partners with Britain. Since Britain was now too weak and impoverished to hold on to its colonies, he reasoned, they must be allowed to go their own ways. Among the first to do so was India.

India had chafed under British rule for decades. Its struggle for independence had been put on hold during the war, throughout which its people remained loyal. Now, however, they wanted their freedom, and Britain, Atlee knew, was in no position to deny them. Within two years of the war's end, the Union Jack came down over Delhi.

As far back as 1908, a viceroy of India, George Curzon, had said that if India were ever lost, then

> your ports and your coaling-stations, your fortresses and your dockyards, your Crown colonies and protectorates will go, too. For either they will be unnecessary, as the tollgates and barbicans of an Empire that has vanished, or they will be taken by an enemy more powerful than yourselves.[39]

Curzon's words were prophetic. Much of the British Empire had been assembled to protect and maintain India, the "jewel in the crown." With the jewel gone, the crown was shabby indeed.

Atlee's government tried to preserve links with the colonies by helping them develop to a point where they could be partners, not in an empire but in a *commonwealth*, a term that had come into general use between the world wars when *empire* was out of favor. It had

Prime Minister Clement Atlee realized that with its failing economy, Britain could no longer maintain its empire.

been called the British Commonwealth, but now began to be referred to as the Commonwealth of Nations. Despite some grumbling by the public, the Labour government, through the Colonial Development and Welfare Act of 1945, pumped money into long-neglected territories, building dams, roads, schools, and hospitals.

Too Little, Too Late

It was too little, too late. In 1942, Gandhi had told U.S. president Franklin Roosevelt, "If India becomes free, the rest will follow."[40] The spirit of nationalism kindled by Gandhi in India had spread throughout what remained of the British Empire. Throughout Africa and the Middle East, rebellions—some violent—broke out that the British, because of a combination of economic weakness and world opinion, could not contain.

By 1957, Britain realized that its economic future lay not in far-flung islands and jungles but across the English Channel in Europe. At first, it held aloof from the new Common Market (now the European Community), then tried to join only to suffer the humiliation of being kept out by France's veto. Finally, in 1973, Britain was admitted. After centuries of colonization, the nation had found a measure of economic security by banding together with its former rivals.

The Weary Titan

THE MOTIVES FOR THE spread of the British Empire were gold, God, and glory. Gold might have been the primary force in empire building, but there were plenty of Britons who cared more about people's souls than their own riches. Their goal—indeed, their mission—was to carry Christian civilization to every corner of the globe. As Colonial Secretary Earl Grey put it in 1853,

> I conceive that, by the acquisition of its Colonial dominions, the Nation has incurred a responsibility of the highest kind, which it is not at liberty to throw off. The authority of the British Crown is at this moment the most powerful instrument, under Providence, of maintaining peace and order in many extensive regions of the earth, and thereby assists in diffusing amongst millions of the human race, the blessings of Christianity and civilization.[41]

Poet Rudyard Kipling referred to this responsibility as "the White Man's Burden,"[42] and for generations men and women were willing to endure all sorts of hardships to take it up. Eventually, however, it became too much. The world was too large, the rivals too numerous, and the empire's nonwhite subjects' desire for freedom too strong for what, after all, was a small nation with limited capabilities. Another poet, Matthew Arnold, captured the mood as early as the 1860s, comparing Britain to a weary Titan:

> Staggering on to her goal;
> Bearing on shoulders immense,
> Atlantean, the load,
> Well-nigh not to be borne,
> Of the too vast orb of her fate.[43]

59

A European missionary poses with two South Pacific converts in this 1845 photograph. Nineteenth-century missionaries hoped to spread their message of Christianity to "uncivilized" territory.

As the challenges of the twentieth century increased, Britons began to wonder if the empire was worth it all. Eventually, they decided that it was not.

Dual Motives

The humanitarian motives of the British colonizers went hand in hand. "We were going as civilisers as well as preachers,"[44] wrote missionary James Stewart in 1874. The reformers looked aghast at such practices as suttee (the Indian practice of burning a widow along with her husband's corpse), cannibalism, plural marriages, and female circumcision. They saw virtually every nonwhite group in the empire as barbarians to be civilized. The British concept of civilization, of course, was Christianity steeped in the tradition of parliamentary government. They thought—as an article of faith—that Britishness could be grafted onto all the various native groups within the empire.

Some imperialists even saw the British economic and civilizing missions as one and the same, as if the bringing of modern technology to remote parts of the world was divinely inspired. Author and clergyman Charles Kingsley said in 1851,

The spinning jenny and the railroad, Cunard's liners and the electric telegraph, are to me . . . signs that we are, on some points at least, in harmony with the universe; that there is a mighty spirit working among us . . . the Ordering and Creating God.[45]

Enduring Hardships

The reformers knew the difficulties of the tasks they took up with such zeal. They knew that the process would take decades, perhaps generations, but their belief that it could eventually be done was un-wavering. "Let us endeavor," said William Wilberforce, a tireless crusader against slavery, "to strike our roots into the soil by the grad-ual introduction and establishment of our own principles and opin-ions [and] above all, as the source of every other improvement, of our religion, and consequently, of our morals."[46]

The problem, of course, was that many of the nonwhite subjects of the empire had no wish to be civilized, at least in British terms. They enjoyed the benefits of empire, particularly the expansion of markets for their products, but they resented the attempts to overthrow

Native Stereotypes

Author G. A. Henty shared the view prevalent among the British im-perialists of the nineteenth century that nonwhites, particularly Africans, were savages to whom it was the duty of white men—namely the British—to bring civilization. In *The British Imperial Expe-rience* by Robert Huttenback, one of Henty's characters is quoted, describing black Africans as

> just like children. . . . They are always laughing and quarreling. They are good-natured and passionate, indolent, but will work hard for a time; clever up to a certain point, densely stupid be-yond. The intelligence of an average negro is about equal to that of a European child of ten years old. A few, a very few, go be-yond this, but these are [an] exception, just as Shakespeare's was an exception to the ordinary intellect of an Englishman. They are fluent talkers, but their ideas are borrowed. They are absolutely without originality, absolutely without inventive power. Living among white men their imitative faculties enable them to attain a considerable amount of civilisation. Left alone to their own devices they retrograde into a state little above their native savagery.

centuries—sometimes millennia—of traditions, traditions that were misunderstood or not understood at all by the British.

An excellent example of such misunderstanding was the introduction in India of rifle cartridges that had been coated with a mixture of pork and beef fat. Since cows were sacred to Hindus and pork was considered unclean by Muslims, the incident touched off a revolt among native troops and led to the great Indian Mutiny of 1857. The attitude of most of the nonwhite subjects of the empire was summed up by Sir Claude Macdonald, who said in 1899, "From the bottom of their hearts they hate us all as the devil hates holy water."[47]

Growing Troubles

Such conflicts occurred frequently throughout the history of the empire, but they were seldom the size of the Indian Mutiny. They generally occurred in remote parts of Africa or far away in the Pacific. In the twentieth century, however, such conflagrations grew larger and gained worldwide attention, much of which did not portray Britain in a favorable light.

Muslim and Hindu mutineers clash with British troops during the Indian Mutiny of 1857.

Eventually, the British began wondering if it was worth all the effort. They not only questioned whether the civilizing mission could be carried out but whether it should even be attempted. Certainly, there was no argument about the abolition of practices such as human sacrifice. But once these were eliminated, a more tolerant generation of colonial administrators began to ask themselves to what extent British, Christian institutions should be exported. After all, Islam was a well-established religion, and Buddhism and Hinduism predated Christianity by hundreds of years. The British way of life, though it seemed to work well for Britain, might not be the best for everyone everywhere. European institutions, wrote future Prime Minister Ramsay MacDonald in 1898, "can no more be carried to India by Englishmen than they can carry ice in their luggage."[48]

Along with the recognition that the British way of life was not necessarily the only correct way came an increased respect for other cultures. The British Empire had been frankly racist. At best, natives were treated as backward children. At worst, they were brutally mistreated. The British had supreme confidence in themselves, but this confidence was too often translated into a derogatory view of everyone else. Poet W. E. Henley wrote, "The world is for one of two races, and of these the English is one."[49]

The empire long paid lip service to the idea of "trusteeship," but the British idea of trusteeship was that the subject people would someday be indistinguishable from Britons except for the color of their skin. As the zeal for reform waned, a movement grew—particularly among members of the Liberal Party—in support of the idea that trusteeship should be based on a respect for native cultures and that to tamper with native traditions was dangerous. Anthropologist Bronislaw Malinowski wrote that cultures were like a cloth "in which all the strands are so closely woven that the destruction of one unmakes the whole."[50]

The Freedom to Leave

From a toleration of "foreign" cultures within the empire, it was only a matter of time before the subject people were given the option of no longer being subjects. Admittedly this was neither quick nor easy. Empire was an ingrained habit that the British were reluctant to give up. Only by constant resistance and worldwide pressure was Britain at last forced to adopt the view of one politician, who said after World War II, "If you are in a place where you are not wanted and where you have not got the force to squash those who don't want you, the only thing to do is to come out."[51]

As the complexity and challenges of the British Empire increased, it seemed to many that the national enthusiasm for governing others dwindled. In the heyday of imperialism, missionaries and administrators endured—for the most part without complaint—severe physical and mental hardships. It was almost a point of pride that service in the colonies involved "long years of exile, a burning sun which dries up the Saxon energies, home sickenings, thankless labour, disease and ofttimes death far from wife, child, friend or kinsman."[52]

Later, fewer Britons were willing to take up the challenge. The earl of Meath helped to establish "Empire Day" as a national holiday to be celebrated on March 24, Queen Victoria's birthday. His goal was to revive and maintain what he regarded as a flagging imperial spirit. Other steps were taken in the hopes of making Britons more physically up to the task. General Robert Baden-Powell was so disappointed in the fitness of the Boer War recruits that he challenged Britain's young people:

> Your forefathers worked hard, fought hard, and died hard to make this empire for you. Don't let them look down from heaven, and see you loafing about with your hands in your pockets, doing nothing to keep it up.[53]

Still, Britain had begun to doubt not only its mission but also its own abilities, and that doubt, wrote historian James Morris, "was a seed that grew with time, to change the nation, the Empire and the world."[54]

The End of Jingo

Britain was also tired of *jingoism*, a word coined to describe the belligerent attitude set forth in the popular music hall song that went,

> We don't want to fight, but, by Jingo, if we do,
> We've got the ships, we've got the men, we've got
>   the money, too.[55]

Indeed, far from being something to avoid, war was thought by some to be an invigorating venture. As one commentator put it in 1898, "Strength is not maintained without exercise."[56]

The Imperial Spirit

As the imperial spirit began to decline in Great Britain, fewer young men came forward than before, eager to take up the cause of spreading Christianity and "civilization" to natives of far-off lands. Ardent imperialists tried to revive that spirit among the nation's youth through a series of patriotic songs, books, and plays.

One such man was G. A. Henty, who had been a war correspondent in the Asante War in Central Africa in the 1870s. During the 1890s Henty turned out a steady stream of books aimed at instilling in young boys the spirit he felt was on the wane. In one such book, *Through the Sikh War,* the young hero is told to consider whether he has what it takes to serve in India. This description of the ideal candidate is found in *The Rise and Fall of the British Empire* by Lawrence James.

> Think it over yourself, Percy. Can you thrash most fellows your own age? Can you run as far and as fast as most of them? Can you take a caning without whimpering over it? Do you feel, in fact, that you are able to go through fully as much as any of your companions? Are you good at planning a piece of mischief, and ready to take the lead in carrying it out? . . . It is pluck and endurance and the downright love of adventure and danger, that have made us the masters of the great part of India, and ere long makes us the rulers of the whole of it.

The Boer War put an end to jingoism. It was difficult to whip up enthusiasm for a conflict in which British troops were humiliated and finally resorted to imprisoning women and children. Imperialists, both in politics and journalism, tried, but the British public was weary of flag waving. "Please understand," Queen Victoria felt compelled to say publicly after a series of British defeats, "there is no one depressed in this house."[57] Victoria's people, however, knew better. Their mood was best expressed by Kipling, who wrote,

> Let us admit it fairly, as a business people should,
> We have had no end of a lesson; it will do us no end of good.
> Not on a single issue, or in one direction or twain,
> But conclusively, comprehensively, and several times and again
> Were all our most holy illusions knocked higher than
>   Gilderoy's kite.
> We've had a jolly good lesson, and it serves us jolly well
>   right![58]

The Lesson Learned

The "jolly good lesson" was that Britain should be wary of armed conflict and imperial expansion. That wariness was reflected by the politicians of the time, notably the members of the Liberal Party. John Morley, secretary for India in the Liberal cabinet of 1905, wrote that, while "nobody means to give anything up," the cabinet would be "in the highest degree jealous both of anything that looks like expansion, extension of protectorates, spheres of influence, and the like; and of anything with the savour of militarism about it."[59] And Lord George Hamilton wrote, "The vast majority of the Cabinet look with apprehension and dislike on any movement or any action which is likely to produce war or disturbance in any part of the British Empire."[60]

The fact was the vast majority of Britons cared far more about what was happening in their own country than in the empire. The issues they were concerned about were taxes and wages, not imperial policy, and they voted in ever-increasing numbers for politicians who agreed with them. Lord Alfred Milner, a former governor of South Africa, lamented his inability to "explain to these damned fools"[61]— the British public—why the empire was good for them.

The aversion to foreign adventure was even stronger after World War I. More than 700,000 men had been killed and the national treasury depleted. The public knew and appreciated the necessity of the war, but they were appalled by the way in which it had been conducted. Novelist George Orwell wrote that "Every junior officer looked on the General Staff as mental defectives" and that "So far as the younger generation was concerned, the official beliefs were dissolving like sand castles."[62] Because of the dreadful carnage of the war and the mood of the survivors, colonial administrators were more difficult to find, and those who were recruited did not share the outlook of those who had preceded them.

Public Ignorance

The vast majority of the British public, battered by war and self-doubt, simply did not care about the empire any longer, and that uncaring attitude was reflected in a profound ignorance. Writer H. G. Wells estimated that "nineteen people out of every twenty . . . knew no more of the empire than they did of the Argentine Republic or the

Italian Renaissance. It did not concern them."[63] It concerned them even less after World War II. According to a poll taken in 1947, half the population could not name a single British possession and 3 percent thought the United States was still a colony.

The empire endured, but the bottom line increasingly was profit and self-interest more than any sort of semidivine mission. John Buchan, who had worked for Milner in South Africa and shared his imperial viewpoint, longed for a "worldwide brotherhood . . . consecrated to the service of peace" but found after the Boer War that

> The historic etiquette was breaking down; in every walk money seemed to count for more; there was a vulgar display of wealth and a *rastaquouère* [unseemly] craze for luxury. I began to have an ugly fear that the empire might decay at the heart.[64]

The day of imperial glory had gone. Those who had shared in that glory saw to their dismay that the values they had cherished were now mocked by a generation made cynical by war and economic hardship and marked, as a Conservative Party member of Parliament said in 1923, "by a habit of disparaging and belittling all British ideas."[65]

There was a new view of glory, that of poet Wilfred Owen, killed during the last week of World War I:

> Not one corner of a foreign field
> But a span as wide as Europe . . .
> An appearance of a titan's grave,
> And the length thereof a thousand miles.
> It crossed all Europe like a mystic Road . . .
> And I heard a voice crying,
> This is the Path of Glory.[66]

The Native
Chapter 6 Peoples

BUFFETED BY WAR AND self-doubt, the British Empire after World War I was like a mighty tree eaten away by disease from the inside. Outwardly, it appeared stronger than ever. In reality, all it needed was a series of strong pushes to send it toppling. Those pushes were provided by native peoples throughout the empire who had little in common except a hunger for freedom.

Rebellions were hardly new to the British, but they had experienced nothing like the groundswell that began in 1919. Reacting to an uprising in Egypt, British foreign secretary Arthur Balfour wrote,

> The Egyptian unrest is doubtless part of a world movement which takes different forms in different places, but is plainly discernible on every continent and in every country. We are only at the beginning of our troubles and it is doubtful whether, and how far, the forces of an orderly civilisation are going to deal effectively with those of social and international disintegration.[67]

Ramsay MacDonald wrote in 1931, "We have all been so distracted by day to day troubles that we never had a chance of surveying the whole situation and hammering out a policy regarding it, but have had to live from agitation to agitation."[68]

Freedom for Ireland

The pattern for the end of the British Empire was established at the place it began—Ireland. Ireland had been an English colony—in whole or in part—since 1174, and the Irish suffered the same eco-

68

nomic and social subjugation that their African or Asian counterparts did. In the decades leading to World War I, the British had often promised "home rule" but never quite got around to granting it.

The Irish grew tired of waiting. In 1916, when Britain was fully occupied with World War I, the *Sinn Féin* ("Ourselves Alone" in Gaelic) Party staged an armed rebellion in Dublin. This so-called Easter Rising didn't amount to much, but it provoked severe reaction by the British. Hundreds of *Sinn Féin* sympathizers were jailed, and sixteen of the leaders were sentenced to death. The British were even callous enough to place a man before a firing squad who had been so badly wounded that he had to be strapped in a chair. Such treatment swung the majority of the Irish people behind *Sinn Féin*. World opinion was solidly against the British, especially in the United States, which was home to millions of Irish immigrants.

The unrest continued after World War I, and the British tried to stamp it out with force. Prime Minister David Lloyd George termed *Sinn Féin* and its military arm, the Irish Republican Army (IRA), a "nest of assassins." The IRA did indeed use terrorist tactics, using car bombs and gunning down British officials. To counter the IRA, the British sent to Ireland the notorious "Black and Tans," a mercenary force so brutal that the situation was inflamed even further.

Residents and police in Coventry, England, survey the damage from an IRA bomb attack in 1939.

The British were like people in quicksand; the harder they fought, the deeper they became entrapped. No matter how many troops they sent, they could not halt the hit-and-run tactics of the IRA. They were learning the truth of what T. E. Lawrence had said years before in Arabia: "You can't make war on a rebellion."[69] At last, they took the only way out, signing a treaty in 1921 that set the stage for Ireland's eventual independence. It was a step the British, especially the Conservative Party imperialists, hated to take because it was like an admission of weakness, but they had to face the reality of their situation.

Gandhi

The events in Ireland had been watched closely throughout the rest of the empire, notably in India and especially by a London-trained lawyer named Mohandas K. Gandhi. It was Gandhi, later known as the Mahatma, or "great soul," who was able to focus a century of discontent and weld it into a mass movement that would not only sweep the British out of India but provide a blueprint that would be followed throughout the century by people seeking justice. The days of the British Empire may have been numbered, but those days—and, indeed, the days of imperialism everywhere—may have been far more numerous had it not been for this outwardly simple yet amazingly complex individual.

Gandhi spent most of his early career in South Africa, working for the rights of Indians there. In an effort to show the British that Indians deserved full citizenship, he organized an ambulance corps during the Boer War and was decorated for valor. After the war, however, the lot of the Indians was no better. Although they contributed much to the economy, principally as traders and merchants, they had no rights of citizenship. Gandhi, an intensely religious man drawing from the Hindu tradition, formulated the concept of satyagraha, or "truth force," a passive, nonviolent technique of resistance designed to convince oppressors of the basic immorality of their oppression.

Gandhi returned to India in 1914. Despite his experience in South Africa, he believed that if Indians supported Britain in World War I, freedom would follow. He was encouraged by the proclamation of Edwin Montagu, secretary of state for India, who said that Britain's policy was one "of increasing association of Indians in every branch of the administration, and the gradual development of self-governing institutions."[70]

The Amritsar Massacre

Again, Gandhi would be disappointed, and the disappointment would be shocking. On April 13, 1919, troops under the command of General Reginald Dyer surrounded a protest gathering in Amritsar that had assembled in defiance of British regulations. At Dyer's order the troops deliberately opened fire. After six minutes of steady shooting, 379 people were killed and about 1,500 wounded. Later, Dyer would say he intended to teach the rebellious Indians a lesson. He succeeded, but not in the way he had hoped.

Gandhi and his colleagues in the Indian National Congress were now convinced that British promises meant nothing, that Britain was determined to hold India by force. He turned the congress, principally a political club for upper-class Indians, into a mass movement that swept the nation.

 Example to the World

Although Great Britain was the largest colonial power, it was not the only one. At the onset of World War II, France, the Netherlands, Portugal, and Italy all had colonies, and even the United States had "possessions," the largest of which was the Philippine Islands. The widespread uprisings of native people in the British Empire gave encouragement to those in other colonies, as historian George Woodcock described in his book *Who Killed the British Empire?*

> The miracle was that the British Empire, which had performed the extraordinary feat of uniting an India that had never been united before, also performed the equally unprecedented feat of giving a common aim of liberation to all its subject peoples. In the past there had been revolts against other empires . . . but these had all been revolts of a single people, and even the great American wave of revolutions that destroyed the Spanish Empire was merely a rebellion of colonial Spaniards against metropolitan Spaniards. . . . What had happened in the British Empire, and spread quickly to the other European Empires, was a simultaneous and sympathetic revolt—usually non-violent but occasionally extremely savage—of people of many languages and cultures against the colonial condition.

Despite the success of the Irish, Gandhi was convinced that the freedom of India could not be won by force. "My ambition," he wrote, "is no less than to convert the British people through non-violence, and thus make them see the wrong they have done India."[71] British goods were boycotted, Indians refused to work for the government, and taxes went unpaid. Thousands, including Gandhi and the congress leaders, were arrested. Rather than resist, they went peacefully. Government and business ground almost to a halt.

The British persisted, but just when it seemed as if Gandhi's influence had passed, they made another blunder. In 1927 a commission was appointed to study possible reforms to the Indian constitution. The Indians welcomed the possibility of reform, but they were stunned when no Indians were named to the commission. One member of Congress called the commission "a deliberate insult to the people of India" that "denies them the right to participate in the determination of the constitution of their own country."[72]

The Salt March

Gandhi's satyagraha movement was reignited. In 1930 he received worldwide attention by leading a protest against a law banning the ownership of any salt not manufactured through a government-owned monopoly. The law kept the price of salt artificially high and made it too expensive for the masses of poor Indians. Wearing only the simple homespun robe of a peasant and carrying a wooden staff, Gandhi undertook a 250-mile march through the countryside to the sea. Only seventy-eight people were with him at the beginning. By the time he arrived in the seaside village of Dandi, many thousands had followed. With reporters and newsreel cameras recording every step, Gandhi walked to the water's edge and ceremoniously picked up a piece of salt, thus breaking the law.

Gandhi's example was followed nationwide, and the British could not ignore the challenge. He and some sixty thousand others were arrested, putting a strain on the legal system and swamping prison facilities. World opinion was solidly against the British, who had no idea how to deal with civil disobedience on such a massive scale. They were, in the words of writer H. G. Wells, like a man who has fallen on an elephant's back "and doesn't know what to do or how to get down."[73]

Mahatma Gandhi leads Indians on a 250-mile march to the sea in protest of Britain's salt production monopoly in India.

Clearly, they had to do something. Gandhi was released from prison and invited to discuss his proposals for more freedom for Indians with the British viceroy, Lord Irwin. The sight of the frail Gandhi in his peasant's garb climbing the stairs of the viceroy's palace symbolized the end of an era. As Indians celebrated, die-hard British imperialists grumbled. Winston Churchill denounced

> the nauseating and humiliating spectacle of this one-time Inner Temple [London's law courts] lawyer, now a seditious fakir [magician], striding half-naked up the steps of the Viceroy's palace there to negotiate and parley on equal terms with the representative of the King-Emperor.[74]

Bowing to the Inevitable

Churchill's world, however, had changed. Even if he did not realize it, others in the British government did. India was becoming ungovernable. Fewer and fewer Britons sought careers in the Indian Civil Service, and their places were taken by Indians. Independence seemed inevitable. To their credit—and possibly because they knew it was impossible—the British did not try to keep India by force as they had Ireland. Instead, they embarked on a slow, often acrimonious, series of negotiations designed to reach the best possible compromise.

Gandhi, Swaraj, and Soul Force

Mohandas Gandhi reduced his goal for India to a single word: *swaraj*, or "freedom." In the early stages of his movement—before the bloody massacre in Amritsar in 1919—he believed that swaraj might be achieved without complete separation from Britain and that it should not result from armed conflict. In 1920, at his urging, the Indian National Congress passed a resolution in favor of swaraj, which Gandhi explained in this passage found in *The Fall of the British Empire* by Colin Cross.

> If the British connection is for the advancement of India, we do not want to destroy it. But if it is inconsistent with our national self-respect, then it is our duty to destroy it. There is room in this resolution for both, those who believe that by retaining the British connection we can purify ourselves and purify the British people, and those who have no such belief. I want you to accompany the carrying of this resolution with a faith and a resolution which nothing on earth can move, that you are intent upon getting "swaraj" at the earliest possible moment, and that you are intent upon getting "swaraj" by means that is legitimate, that is honourable, and by means that is non-violent, that is peaceful. You have resolved upon this thing that so far as we can see today we cannot give battle to this Government [the British] by means of steel, but we can give battle by exercising what is often called soul force.

Britain's forbearance paid off when, despite past injustices, the vast majority of Indians supported the Allies during World War II. When the British viceroy of India proclaimed a state of war against Japan, Jawaharlal Nehru, Gandhi's chief lieutenant, complained that his people had never been consulted and that there was "something rotten when one man . . . could plunge 400 million human beings into war without the slightest reference to them."[75] However, neither he nor Gandhi could bring themselves to support Japan. "We do not seek our independence out of British ruin,"[76] Gandhi said.

After the war, Gandhi's methods finally won out. Indian independence came swiftly. The British saw the necessity for maintaining good relations with India. As Viceroy Archibald Wavell wrote in 1944,

> If we can secure India as a friendly partner in the British Commonwealth our predominant influence in these countries [of Asia] will, I think, be assured; with a lost and hostile India, we

are likely to be reduced in the East to the position of commercial bag-men [itinerant salesmen].[77]

Parting Between Friends

The British had learned a valuable lesson. By cooperating, however
reluctantly, with a native population determined on freedom, they
had gained an ally, whereas their brutal tactics in Ireland had earned
them an eternal enemy. When independence for India finally came,
the last viceroy, Lord Louis Mountbatten, was able to call it "a parting between friends, who have learned to honour and respect one another, even in disagreement."[78]

Gandhi's influence and his teaching of nonviolent resistance
went far beyond the borders of India, which was what he intended.
"My ambition is higher than independence," he said as early as 1928.
"Through the deliverance of India I seek to deliver the so-called
weaker races from the crushing heels of Western exploitation in
which England is the greatest partner."[79]

*British viceroy Lord Louis Mountbatten (second from right) negotiates
India's independence with the future president of India, Nehru (far left), in
1947.*

Respect for an Opponent

Although they resisted the movement led by Mohandas Gandhi, most of the British establishment had the highest respect for Gandhi as an individual. The British had encountered resistance and rebellion before, but they found that dealing with the saintly, peaceful Gandhi was far different, and far more difficult, than with an armed uprising. The British dilemma was summed up by C. N. Broomfield, the judge in Gandhi's trial in 1922. It is found in *End of Empire* by Brian Lapping:

> Mr. Gandhi, you have made my task easier in one way by pleading guilty to the charge. Nevertheless, what remains, namely the determination of a just sentence, is perhaps as difficult a proposition as a judge in this country could have to face. . . . You are in a different category from any person I have ever tried or am likely to have to try. . . . In the eyes of millions of your countrymen, you are a great patriot and a great leader. Even those who differ from you in politics look upon you as a man of high ideals and of noble and even saintly life. It is my duty to judge you as a man subject to the law who has, by his own admission, broken the law and committed what to an ordinary man must appear to be grave offences against the state. I do not forget that you have constantly preached against violence and that you have . . . done much to prevent violence.

After sentencing Gandhi to six years in prison, Broomfield added, "If the course of events in India should make it possible for the Government to reduce the period and release you, no one will be better pleased than I."

Even before Gandhi's methods brought independence to India, they were taken up in Africa. In 1945 a group of then-unknown African leaders met at a Pan-African Congress in Manchester, England. They passed a resolution to "demand for Black Africa autonomy and independence."[80] They agreed that their tactics would be those of Gandhi but that violence might be used as a last resort.

The organizer of the conference was Kwame Nkrumah. Born in the Gold Coast and educated in Pennsylvania, Nkrumah had studied the works of Karl Marx and Lenin and the career of Marcus Garvey, the leader of an African American nationalist movement in the United States. He was determined to re-create in Africa what was nearing completion in India.

The Accra Riots

In 1947, Nkrumah returned to his native country as secretary of the United Gold Coast Convention (UGCC), a native organization led by Dr. J. B. Danquah and dedicated to seeking self-government through constitutional means. Shortly thereafter, as in Ireland and India, a single incident sent events in another direction. In February 1948, ex-servicemen seeking back pay marched on the British governor's residence in Accra. There was a confrontation with police, two of the marchers were shot to death, and rioting spread throughout the city.

Thinking that the UGCC was behind the riots, the governor, Sir Gerald Creasy, ordered that its leaders, including Danquah and Nkrumah, be arrested. Until this incident, the people of the Gold Coast cared little about the UGCC. The arrest of the leaders, however, made them heroes.

Creasy asked the London government to declare a state of emergency. Matters could have disintegrated into another Ireland had it not been for two far-sighted administrators, Colonial Secretary

Inspired by Gandhi's movement for justice in India, Kwame Nkrumah dedicated himself to gaining independence for the Gold Coast.

Arthur Creech Jones and his deputy Andrew Cohen. They believed
that British interests in Africa would best be served by training
Africans to run their own countries. The Gold Coast gave them an
opportunity to show how it could be done.

They appointed a British judge, Aiken Watson, to conduct an inquiry. Watson's report showed how far British thinking had come.
Merely allowing Africans representation in a legislature, he wrote,

> provided no outlet for a people eagerly emerging into political
> consciousness. . . . The constitution and government must be re-
> shaped as to give every African of ability an opportunity to help
> govern the country. . . . In all appointments or promotions in the
> public services the first question to be asked is: "Is there an
> African capable of filling the appointment?"[81]

A new governor, Sir Charles Arden-Clarke, was appointed, and
an all-African committee was formed to make recommendations on
reforms. Arden-Clarke and Danquah favored a moderate approach,
but they reckoned without Nkrumah, who wanted nothing less than
complete independence.

Positive Action

Nkrumah formed his own party, the Convention People's Party, and announced a program, Positive Action, based on Gandhi's principles. A
general strike and boycott began on January 8, 1950. Despite Nkrumah's
orders, however, scattered violence broke out, and Arden-Clarke used
this as an excuse to imprison Nkrumah. With Nkrumah behind bars,
Arden-Clarke continued to work with Danquah, and a general election,
the first ever in black Africa, was scheduled for February 1951.

Danquah might have been preferred by Arden-Clarke, but
Nkrumah had captured the backing of the people. A loophole in the
election law allowed Nkrumah to be a candidate even though he was
in prison. He was elected by a twenty-to-one majority, and his party
claimed thirty-four of the thirty-eight seats in the new legislature.

Arden-Clarke was at a crossroads. Other colonial governors in earlier times might have invalidated the election. Arden-Clarke, however,
demonstrated the attitude that would eventually prevail throughout the
empire. He bowed to the will of the people. Nkrumah was released
from prison and invited to the governor's palace. Mutual suspicion

quickly turned into respect and even affection. Nkrumah later wrote that Arden-Clarke was "a man with a strong sense of justice and fair play, with whom I could easily be friends."[82]

Working together, Arden-Clarke and Nkrumah supervised the transformation of the colony of the Gold Coast to the independent republic of Ghana. It was the way of the future but still was highly unpopular in Conservative Party circles. Creech Jones, Cohen, and Arden-Clarke, however, knew that it was inevitable.

The Suez War

There would be many more nationalist movements throughout the empire, not all of them as amicably solved as that in Ghana. The British occasionally reverted to force, as in Cyprus and in Egypt following the seizure of the Suez Canal in 1956 by Gamal Nasser, an army officer who had overthrown the Egyptian monarchy and was seeking to free his country from British control. World opinion was on the side of the Egyptians. The United States flatly refused to support Britain as long as the British tried to put military pressure on Nasser. Britain was forced to order a humiliating withdrawal.

Nkrumah reads a dispatch from Britain announcing independence for the Gold Coast in 1956.

The era of imperial might had come to an end. For the rest of the century, when the various peoples of the British Empire, now officially the Commonwealth, sought their freedom, Britain gave it to them. Sometimes they were not ready for it. Sometimes anarchy and mass murder by rival native groups followed the British exit, but the British now knew they could not dictate the pace of freedom. As Arden-Clarke wrote about Ghana,

> A powerful body of opinion in the highest quarters here [London] think that I am going too far and too fast but as no one has been able to put forward an alternative policy that has the remotest prospect of working, I am being allowed to have my way. . . . They forget you cannot slow down a flood—the best you can hope to do is to keep the torrent within its proper channel.[83]

Chapter 7 Sunset

O NE BY ONE THE various elements of the British Empire broke away. First it was a drip, then another, then a trickle, and finally a flood. Some went amiably, retaining contact with Britain through the amorphous collection of nations known as the Commonwealth. Others went violently. By the end of the twentieth century all that remained of the empire that once encompassed a quarter of the globe were a handful of islands and the lone mainland outpost of Gibraltar.

Among the first elements to go was the very name "British Empire." After World War I, colonial empires were out of fashion. Even though European nations continued to grab territory, the new acquisitions were called "protectorates" or "mandates," even though they were ruled as completely as any colony. In addition, the British-settled dominions such as Canada and Australia had been demanding and receiving more autonomy and clearly had no wish to be part of anyone's "empire."

A series of imperial conferences in the 1920s weakened the hold that Britain had on the dominions. The chief representatives of Britain in the dominions were the governors-general. They held considerable power, although nowhere near as much as the Indian viceroys. Traditionally, they had been appointed by the Crown after being nominated by the British government. In 1926, however, the power of nominating the governors-general was transferred to the prime minister of each dominion, thereby limiting London's control. In 1930, the assembled prime ministers approved a declaration stating that the dominions were "autonomous communities within the British Empire . . . in no way subordinate to each other . . . though united by

The Commonwealth Concept

After World War I, it was clear that the concept of the "settlement" colonies such as Canada and Australia being subordinates in a British "Empire" was outmoded. To create a new structure that would formalize the degree of independence achieved by the white dominions, the term *commonwealth* was used.

The term had been used for the brief period of time that England was a republic in the 1600s, and it was revived in 1884 when future prime minister Lord Rosebery spoke to an Australian audience. The most forceful speaker for the creation of the British Commonwealth was Jan Smuts, the prime minister of South Africa, who said in 1917 (as quoted in Colin Cross's *The Fall of the British Empire*):

> "Empire" is misleading, because it makes people think we are one community, to which the word "Empire" can appropriately be applied. . . . We are a system of States, and not a stationary system, but a dynamic and evolving system, always going forward to new destinies. . . . Here you have the United Kingdom with a number of Crown Colonies. Beside that you have a large Protectorate like Egypt. . . . Then you have a great Dependency, like India. . . . These are enormous problems, but beyond them we come to the so-called Dominions, independent in their government, which have been evolved on the principles of the free constitutional system into almost independent States, which all belong to this community of nations, and which I prefer to call "The British Commonwealth of Nations."

a common allegiance to the Crown . . . as members of the British Commonwealth of Nations."[84]

The Statute of Westminster

A year later the declaration was incorporated into the Statute of Westminster, passed by Parliament, which gave the "white" dominions—Canada, Australia, New Zealand, South Africa, Newfoundland (not yet a part of Canada), and Ireland (which still had a slight legal connection to Britain)—complete independence. Britain could no longer dictate to them, even on matters of foreign policy. They were free to leave the Commonwealth, which Ireland soon did.

Although in 1931 the Commonwealth was confined to the "white" dominions, it would later serve as a framework for nonwhite colonies to retain a connection with Britain as they gained independence. After

World War II, the word *British* was dropped, as was the term *dominion*. Eventually, allegiance to the British monarchy no longer was required, and the Commonwealth became a loose federation that declined in importance as Britain became more interested in the Common Market, later known as the European Community.

The Commonwealth was opened to nonwhites after World War II when India finally won its long battle for freedom. Labour Party prime minister Clement Atlee, who ousted Conservative Winston Churchill in 1945, was determined to transfer all power to the Indians at the earliest possible date. The man he chose to effect the transfer was Earl Louis Mountbatten, a cousin of King George VI.

Deadline for Freedom

Mountbatten made it clear from the day he assumed office as viceroy in March 1947 that he was committed to a free India—not a vague "sometime" in the future but no later than June 1948. "All this is yours," he told Gandhi as they walked through the gardens of the viceroy's palace. "We are only trustees. We have come to make it over to you."[85]

Mountbatten was as good as his word. In fact, when it became clear to him that there would have to be two independent states—India for the Hindus and Pakistan for the Muslim minority—he accelerated the process. At midnight on August 14, the Union Jack was lowered for the last time. Ceremonies in Karachi, Pakistan, on the

Upon assuming office as viceroy, Mountbatten announced his commitment to ending British rule in India.

Independence Day in India

A formal, dignified ceremony had been planned to inaugurate the new independent state of India on August 15, 1947. Those plans had to be abandoned because of the huge, enthusiastic crowd that turned out—a crowd that was far larger than had been anticipated.

The public square was packed so tightly that the bands could not play. The viceroy, Lord Louis Mountbatten, could not get from his carriage to the platform erected for speeches so he simply signaled for the Indian flag to be raised. In a later report to the British government, Mountbatten described the scene (quoted in *End of Empire* by Brian Lapping):

> Danger of a large-scale accident was becoming so great that we decided the only thing to do was to move the state coach on and draw the crowd with us. For this reason I invited [future Indian prime minister Jawaharlal] Nehru to stay in the coach, which he did, sitting like a schoolboy on the front hood above the seats. Meanwhile refugees who had fainted or had been almost crushed under the wheels were pulled on board and we ended with four Indian ladies and their children, the Polish wife of a British officer and an Indian pressman [reporter] who crawled up behind. The bodyguard gradually opened a way through the crowd and then the whole throng began to follow us. Hundreds of thousands of people all running together is an impressive sight; several thousand ran the whole three miles back alongside the coach and behind it, being stopped finally by the police only at the gates of Government House.

14th and in Delhi, India, on the 15th marked the entry of two new members of the Commonwealth amid an outpouring of both patriotism and pro-British feeling. An Indian journalist wrote that cheering crowds carried British officers on their shoulders.

> It seemed that a hundred and fifty years of bitterness, the massacre at Amritsar, all the civil disobedience movements and all the anti-British feeling had totally vanished and this nation had become more pro-British than it had ever been since the British came.[86]

The Religious Wars

The departure of the British opened a sad chapter in the decline of the empire. India and Pakistan might have felt kindly toward the British, but they hated each other. The British pullout unleashed an ethnic war in which an estimated 200,000 people were killed. In years to come, other religious and ethnic hatreds would flare up in former colonies when the British flag came down.

Such was the case in Palestine, entrusted to British rule after World War I. The difference was that, in addition to hating one another, the Jews and Arabs of Palestine hated the British as well. British attempts to appease the Arabs by limiting Jewish immigration from Europe into Palestine after World War II outraged world opinion, especially coming on the heels of the slaughter of millions of Jews in Nazi Germany. At the same time, the Arabs felt the British were conceding too much to the Jews.

As guerrilla warfare against their troops intensified and their policy of trying to hold on to Palestine was scorned even at home, the British gave up. They dumped the problem in the lap of the United Nations, which voted in November 1947 to partition Palestine into a Jewish and an Arab state. The British began withdrawing troops, the last of which left on May 14, 1948. Four days later the Jews proclaimed the nation of Israel.

Palestine was not the only loss to the empire in 1948. With India free, Burma was now no longer needed to defend it and was allowed to leave in 1948. Malaysia and Ghana completed their peaceful transitions to independence in 1957. The only other possession to achieve freedom in the 1950s was Sudan, which was rushed into freedom in 1956 by the British in order to keep it from being snapped up by Egypt's Nasser.

Decade of Conflict

Sudan's independence, far from being a sign of Britain's desire to divest itself of the empire, came when the Conservative Party regained control of the government and renewed a policy of trying to hold on by force. There were three major areas of conflict in the 1950s: Kenya, Egypt, and Cyprus. The uprising of the "Mau Mau" faction of the Kikuyu tribe in Kenya was the most violent of any in Africa. Although the goal of the Mau Mau was freedom from Britain, most of their violence was directed primarily at other Africans who would not join them. The British, however, were the targets in Cyprus and Egypt, and the outcome showed how frail Britain's power had become.

In 1952, the British-backed Egyptian monarchy was overthrown by a group of army officers headed by Colonel Gamal Nasser. Nasser was determined to end the British military presence in Egypt but was willing to compromise. The Anglo-Egyptian Treaty of 1954 called for the withdrawal of British troops from the Suez Canal Zone by 1956, but the canal itself would still be operated by a British-French company. On July 15, 1956, however, Nasser suddenly announced that the company had been nationalized and that the canal would be operated by the Egyptian government.

British prime minister Anthony Eden reacted forcefully, thinking—without any real evidence—that the British would be denied the use of the canal. He formulated a clumsy scheme, secretly inducing Israel to attack Egypt from the east. This would give Britain and France an excuse to launch a "peacekeeping" invasion and re-

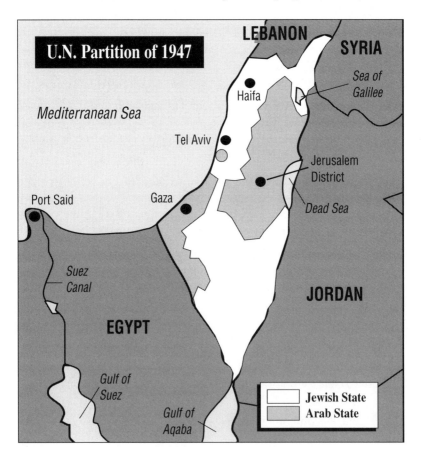

Colonel Gamal Nasser (seated, far left) and his army officers led a military coup that overthrew the British-backed Egyptian monarchy in 1952. Seated at far right is Anwar Sadat, who later went on to become president of Egypt. President Sadat was assassinated in 1982.

gain control of the canal. The operation collapsed in the face of strong opposition from the United States, and the British invasion force was withdrawn. Nothing could have better illustrated Britain's weakness, and a member of Parliament said that Britain had no choice but "to admit to the world that we are now an American satellite."[87]

War in Cyprus

The weakness was underscored in Cyprus, where the British faced a grimly determined freedom movement led militarily by Colonel Georgios Grivas and politically by Archbishop Makarios III. With Palestine gone and their withdrawal from Egypt looming, the British were determined to hold on to Cyprus to maintain a presence in the Middle East. An official at the Colonial Office proclaimed that "nothing less than continued sovereignty over this island can enable Britain to carry out her strategic obligations to Europe, the Mediterranean and the Middle East."[88]

Eventually, the British had thirty thousand troops on Cyprus, an island about the size of Puerto Rico, but the war dragged on. It was an ugly conflict, reminiscent in some ways of the Boer War. The civilian population sided with and protected the rebels, and the

Children in a Cyprus village peer across barbed wire at British soldiers, stationed there to quell the freedom movement by rebel leaders.

British imprisoned hundreds of civilians in concentration camps, allegedly torturing some to elicit information. Finally, in 1957, after three years of fruitless warfare, the British had had enough. Makarios, who had been arrested and exiled, was invited to return, and negotiations were begun that would result in the independence of Cyprus in 1960.

Cyprus was Britain's last large-scale imperial military venture, and the man who ended it and ushered in a new era was Prime Minister Harold Macmillan. Macmillan had been a staunch supporter of the war in Cyprus, but he saw that conflict, coupled with the Suez crisis in Egypt, ruin both the health and political career of his predecessor, Eden. Moreover, he could see that the policy of trying to hang on to the remnants of the empire was ruining the health of his country as well. Morale was low and military expenditures were high, far too high for an economy still feeling the adverse effects of World War II.

Macmillan's Vision

An astute politician, Macmillan saw that the future of Great Britain lay not in continuing as if Queen Victoria were still alive but in adapting as best it could to a changing world. The colonies, long ago an economic engine to Britain, now were like an anchor around its neck. British industry had long since realized this and had reduced colonial investments. Britain's economic future, both the business community and Macmillan saw, was in the new European Common Market.

In 1960, in a speech in South Africa, Macmillan articulated Britain's new approach. It was one of the most important speeches ever given by a British statesman, and with it the British Empire came to an end.

> Ever since the break-up of the Roman Empire one of the most constant facts of political life in Europe has been the emergence of independent nations. They have come into existence over the centuries in different shapes with different forms of government. But all have been inspired with a keen feeling of nationalism, which has grown as the nations have grown.
>
> In the twentieth century, and especially since the end of the war, the processes which gave birth to the nation-states of Europe have been repeated all over the world. We have seen the awakening of a national consciousness in peoples who have lived for centuries in dependence on some other power.
>
> Fifteen years ago this movement spread through Asia. Many countries there of different races and civilisations pressed their claims to an independent national life. Today the same thing is happening in Africa. The most striking of all the impressions I have formed since I left London a month ago is of the strength of this African national consciousness. In different places it may take different forms, but it is happening everywhere. The wind of change is blowing through the continent.[89]

Aiding Independence

Macmillan saw what Creech Jones and Cohen had seen ten years earlier: that it was in Britain's best interest not to stand in the way of native nationalism, or even to stand by and watch it, but to actively assist in the quest for independence. In Nyasaland, where an independence movement led by Hastings Banda had been suppressed and Banda imprisoned, Macmillan sent a high court judge, Sir Patrick Devlin, to make an official inquiry. Devlin reported that British authorities were running what amounted to a police state. Banda was released and later became the first president of what was renamed Malawi.

In Kenya, site of the Mau Mau terrorism, Kikuyu leader Jomo Kenyatta was freed from prison. With the help of Malcolm Mac-Donald, a governor appointed by Macmillan, Kenyatta's party won a majority in a 1963 election, and he was made prime minister. White settlers feared a new wave of terrorism similar to the Mau Mau uprising of the previous decade, but Kenyatta's moderation astounded them. To a meeting of white farmers he said,

> You have something to forget, just as I have. This has been worrying many of you; but let me tell you Jomo Kenyatta has no intention of retaliating or looking backwards. We are going to forget the past and look forward to the future. I have suffered imprisonment and detention; but that is gone and I am not going to remember it. . . . Many of you are as Kenyan as myself . . . let us join hands and work for the benefit of Kenya, not for the benefit of one particular community.[90]

The End Comes Swiftly

The trickle had become a flood. Every year saw at least one and sometimes four or five former colonies granted independence. Zanzibar and Tanganyika merged to form Tanzania. Bechuanaland became Botswana. Northern Rhodesia became Zambia. Soon, not a single British possession remained where once a person could have gone from Cape Town to Cairo without leaving British soil.

In the Americas, British Guiana became independent Guyana in 1966 after 330 years of British rule. British Honduras followed as Belize. Jamaica, the Bahamas, and a host of other islands became nations.

In 1964 Malta joined Cyprus in independence, and Britain was out of the Mediterranean—except for Gibraltar—for the first time since 1798. Likewise, the British presence in the Middle East came to an end with the sovereignty of Kuwait, Qatar, Bahrain, and Aden.

In Asia, Singapore, North Borneo, and Sarawak joined Malaya in 1963 to form Malaysia. Papua New Guinea became independent in 1975, and the British Solomon Islands became independent three years later. The final piece of Britannia in Asia passed into history in 1997 when Hong Kong was returned to China under the terms of a lease signed in 1898.

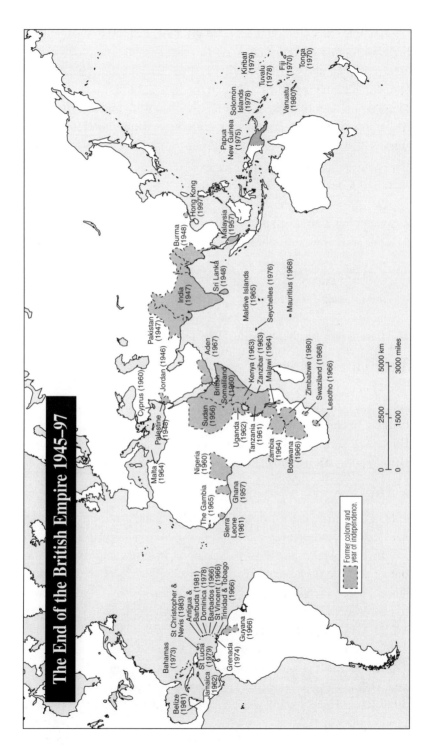

The End of the British Empire 1945–97

Former colony and year of independence.

Except for Gibraltar and a few small, scattered islands, the British Empire had vanished. With it went the age of empire. For the most part, it had been a friendly parting. The former colonies retained emotional ties to Britain, and the British remembered the empire—when they thought of it at all—with nostalgia, tempered by a realization that it could not have endured. As Kipling had foreseen a century before,

> Far-called, our navies melt away;
> On due and headland sinks the first:
> Lo, all our pomp of yesterday
> Is one with Nineveh and Tyre![91]

Echoes of

Empire

N THE HEYDAY OF European empires, it was customary to make colonial possessions on world maps the same color as the mother country. Red was the traditional color for Great Britain and the many parts of its empire. At the end of the twentieth century, the once-huge red area—including Canada, Australia, India, and half of Africa—was reduced to Britain itself and a few scattered dots.

What had it all meant? The question was posed in 1960 to a British colonial official in Nigeria on the eve of independence. It means, he said, that "tomorrow morning I suppose I'll have to brush my own teeth." [92]

The British Empire meant a great deal more, however, to the far-flung lands once under the Union Jack. For one thing, there were the tangible, in some cases permanent, remnants of British rule. The new republics were held together by networks of roads and bridges, sustained by farms made possible by dams and waterways. People worked in factories that existed because of British investors, and their goods found a worldwide market through the Commonwealth.

The greatest unifying factor, however, far more so than highways and bridges, was the English language. English was often the only vehicle of communication through which the Hindi-speaking doctor in Delhi could speak with his Bengali-speaking colleague and through which the Nigerian speakers of Igbo, Hausa, and Yoruba could converse.

The Legal System

Along with their language, the British brought their systems of government and justice. The British doctrine of common law and the

93

court system were adopted; even the red robe and powdered wig of the judge in London could be seen everywhere from Malaya to Montreal. In many countries, parliamentary democracy, complete with political parties, was retained, although several lapsed into dictatorships.

Another British legacy, though not always an enduring one, was religion. The reformers were sincere in their desire to bring Christianity to the people of the empire. They did not succeed to any great extent in areas that already had established major religions, such as Islam in Sudan or Hinduism in India, but they had a great impact on black Africa. As a result of the empire, Anglicanism—the churches derived from the Church of England—is a force worldwide, and many of its most effective and distinguished leaders, such as South African bishop Desmond Tutu, are nonwhite.

Less tangible, but probably more important, were the effects of the introduction of European culture. The British brought with them a way of life, a value system that they attempted—with the best of motives—to graft onto the cultures they found. Those cultures were undeniably damaged as a result, but the imperial experience—for good or ill—prepared the former colonies to take their places in a modern world.

Borrowing the Best

Not everything the British brought to their colonies was positive. The empire was largely racist and oftentimes unfeeling or even cruel to those it governed. But many peoples were able to take the best parts—the Christian moral outlook, the belief in individual rights, that most British of ideologies known as "fair play"—and combine them with elements of their own cultures to form progressive national outlooks that were both Old World and New. As South African leader Nelson Mandela said,

> You must remember that I was brought up in a British school, and at the time Britain was the home of everything that was best in the world. I have not discarded the influence which Britain and British culture exercised on us.[93]

Kipling's captains and kings departed, and the British Empire, indeed, was one with ancient Nineveh and Tyre. It had left behind a

Christianity became an established religion in many parts of the empire, especially in Africa. One of Anglicanism's most respected leaders today is South African bishop Desmond Tutu.

legacy far more enduring than bridges or factories, however. Generations of British settlers, missionaries, fortune hunters, and governors had lived, worked, and many times died trying to make their part of the earth a better place. Their motives often were not the noblest, their methods often were not the most humane, but their zeal transformed a large part of the world.

Outside Kohima in modern-day Bangladesh stands a memorial. The inscription was written to denote the sacrifice of British soldiers to the mother country, but it could apply equally to the contributions of the empire:

When you go home, tell them of us and say
For your tomorrows we gave our today.[94]

Notes

Introduction: Land of Hope and Glory

1. Quoted in Bernard Porter, *The Lion's Share*. London: Longman Group, 1975, p. 44.
2. Quoted in Porter, *The Lion's Share*, p. 45.
3. Quoted in Colin Cross, *The Fall of the British Empire: 1918–1968*. New York: Coward McCann, 1968, p. 17.

Chapter 1: Sunrise

4. Quoted in Lawrence James, *The Rise and Fall of the British Empire*. New York: St. Martin's Press, 1994, p. 217.
5. Quoted in James, *The Rise and Fall of the British Empire*, p. 290.
6. Quoted in Robert Hughes, *The Fatal Shore*. New York: Alfred A. Knopf, 1987, p. 277.
7. Quoted in James, *The Rise and Fall of the British Empire*, p. 210.

Chapter 2: The Changing World Order

8. Quoted in Paul Halsall, editor, Internet Modern History Sourcebook, www.fordham.edu/halsall/mod/rulebritannia.html.
9. Quoted in Porter, *The Lion's Share,* p. 114.
10. Quoted in Porter, *The Lion's Share,* p. 76.
11. Quoted in Porter, *The Lion's Share,* p. 102.
12. Quoted in James Morris, *Pax Britannica: The Climax of Empire*. New York: Harcourt, Brace & World, 1968, p. 492.
13. Quoted in Porter, *The Lion's Share,* p. 308.
14. Quoted in James, *The Rise and Fall of the British Empire*, p. 318.
15. Quoted in Porter, *The Lion's Share,* p. 123.

Chapter 3: Victory's Bitter Fruits

16. Quoted in Porter, *The Lion's Share*, p. 175.

17. Quoted in William Manchester, *Visions of Glory*, vol. 1 of *The Last Lion: Winston Spencer Churchill.* New York: Dell, 1983, p. 222.
18. Porter, *The Lion's Share,* p. 178.
19. Quoted in Brian Lapping, *End of Empire.* New York: St. Martin's Press, 1985, p. 36.
20. Quoted in Porter, *The Lion's Share,* p. 240.
21. Quoted in Porter, *The Lion's Share,* p. 243.
22. Quoted in James, *The Rise and Fall of the British Empire*, p. 361.
23. Quoted in Lapping, *End of Empire,* p. 105.
24. Quoted in Porter, *The Lion's Share,* p. 245.
25. Quoted in Cross, *The Fall of the British Empire,* p. 232.
26. Quoted in Porter, *The Lion's Share,* p. 307.
27. Quoted in James, *The Rise and Fall of the British Empire,* p. 500.
28. Quoted in Porter, *The Lion's Share,* p. 112.

Chapter 4: The Cost of Conquest

29. Quoted in James, *The Rise and Fall of the British Empire*, p. 6.
30. Quoted in Paul Kennedy, *The Rise and Fall of the Great Powers.* New York: Vantage Books, 1989, p. 151.
31. Quoted in Morris, *Pax Britannica,* p. 102.
32. Quoted in Cross, *The Fall of the British Empire,* p. 27.
33. Quoted in Morris, *Pax Britannica,* p. 109.
34. Quoted in James, *The Rise and Fall of the British Empire,* p. 216.
35. Quoted in Porter, *The Lion's Share,* p. 3.
36. Quoted in James Morris, *Farewell the Trumpets: An Imperial Retreat.* New York: Harcourt Brace Jovanovich, 1978, p. 93.
37. Quoted in Porter, *The Lion's Share,* p. 264.
38. Quoted in James, *The Rise and Fall of the British Empire,* p. 458.
39. Quoted in George Woodcock, *Who Killed the British Empire?* New York: Quadrangle/New York Times Book Co., 1974, p. 301.
40. Quoted in Morris, *Farewell the Trumpets,* p. 495.

Chapter 5: The Weary Titan

41. Quoted in Porter, *The Lion's Share,* p. 14.
42. Quoted in Morris, *Pax Britannica,* p. 122.
43. Quoted in Morris, *Farewell the Trumpets,* p. 91.
44. Quoted in James, *The Rise and Fall of the British Empire,* p. 188.

45. Quoted in Kennedy, *The Rise and Fall of the Great Powers*, p. 158.
46. Quoted in Porter, *The Lion's Share*, p. 19.
47. Quoted in Porter, *The Lion's Share*, p. 158.
48. Quoted in Porter, *The Lion's Share*, p. 292.
49. Quoted in Porter, *The Lion's Share*, p. 128.
50. Quoted in Porter, *The Lion's Share*, p. 293.
51. Quoted in Morris, *Farewell the Trumpets*, p. 496.
52. Quoted in Porter, *The Lion's Share*, p. 44.
53. Quoted in James, *The Rise and Fall of the British Empire*, p. 330.
54. Morris, *Farewell the Trumpets*, p. 99.
55. Quoted in Morris, *Pax Britannica*, p. 115.
56. Quoted in Porter, *The Lion's Share*, p. 129.
57. Quoted in Morris, *Farewell the Trumpets*, p. 99.
58. Quoted in Morris, *Farewell the Trumpets*, p. 98.
59. Quoted in Porter, *The Lion's Share*, p. 205.
60. Quoted in Morris, *Farewell the Trumpets*, p. 125.
61. Quoted in Porter, *The Lion's Share*, p. 193.
62. Quoted in Porter, *The Lion's Share*, p. 256.
63. Quoted in Porter, *The Lion's Share*, p. 284.
64. Quoted in Porter, *The Lion's Share*, p. 230.
65. Quoted in Porter, *The Lion's Share*, p. 283.
66. Quoted in Morris, *Farewell the Trumpets*, p. 200.

Chapter 6: The Native Peoples

67. Quoted in James, *The Rise and Fall of the British Empire*, p. 371.
68. Quoted in Kennedy, *The Rise and Fall of the Great Powers*, p. 333.
69. Quoted in James, *The Rise and Fall of the British Empire*, p. 381.
70. Quoted in Cross, *The Fall of the British Empire*, p. 63.
71. Quoted in Woodcock, *Who Killed the British Empire?*, p. 249.
72. Quoted in Porter, *The Lion's Share*, p. 297.
73. Quoted in Morris, *Farewell the Trumpets*, p. 285.
74. Quoted in Cross, *The Fall of the British Empire*, p. 196.
75. Quoted in Morris, *Farewell the Trumpets*, p. 477.
76. Quoted in Robert A. Huttenback, *The British Imperial Experience*. New York: Harper and Row, 1966, p. 191.
77. Quoted in Lapping, *End of Empire*, p. 61.

78. Quoted in Morris, *Farewell the Trumpets*, p. 491.

79. Quoted in Woodcock, *Who Killed the British Empire?*, p. 314.

80. Quoted in Cross, *The Fall of the British Empire*, p. 362.

81. Quoted in Lapping, *End of Empire*, p. 371.

82. Quoted in Lapping, *End of Empire*, p. 378.

83. Quoted in Lapping, *End of Empire*, p. 382.

Chapter 7: Sunset

84. Quoted in Morris, *Farewell the Trumpets*, p. 335.

85. Quoted in Morris, *Farewell the Trumpets*, p. 485.

86. Quoted in Lapping, *End of Empire*, p. 91.

87. Quoted in James, *The Rise and Fall of the British Empire*, p. 585.

88. Quoted in Porter, *The Lion's Share*, p. 327.

89. Quoted in Cross, *The Fall of the British Empire*, p. 343.

90. Quoted in Lapping, *End of Empire*, p. 442.

91. Quoted in James, *The Rise and Fall of the British Empire*, p. 216.

Epilogue: Echoes of Empire

92. Quoted in Lapping, *End of Empire*, p. 2.

93. Quoted in James, *The Rise and Fall of the British Empire*, p. 629.

94. Quoted in James, *The Rise and Fall of the British Empire*, p. 556.

Chronology

1600
Merchants establish the British East India Company.

1607
Britain establishes Jamestown Colony in Virginia.

1610
Newfoundland becomes a British colony.

1623
Barbados becomes the first British colony in the West Indies; British expelled from East Indies by Dutch, then turn attention to India.

1757
Robert Clive engineers revolt in Indian kingdom of Bengal; British take control from native rulers.

1761
British defeat French in India at the Battle of Pondicherry.

1763
British occupy most of Canada as a result of the French and Indian War.

1770
British colonize Australia..

1776
July 4: American colonies declare independence.

1788
British colonize New Zealand.

1806
British capture Cape Colony of South Africa.

1815
British defeat Napoleon Bonaparte and become unrivaled as a world power.

1819
British lease island of Singapore.

1823
The United States bars European intervention in the Americas with the Monroe Doctrine.

1839
British colonize Aden.

1854–1856
Britain blocks Russian expansion in Crimean War.

1857
Native troops mutiny against British in India.

1869
French open Suez Canal in Egypt.

1871
Chancellor Otto von Bismarck unifies Germany.

1875
British buy part interest in Suez Canal.

1877
Britain annexes the Orange Free State and the Transvaal.

1878
British annex the island of Cyprus in the Mediterranean Sea; Afghans defeat invasion by British.

1879
British successfully invade Afghanistan.

1882
British invade Egypt and take control of Suez Canal.

1884
British establish colony in Somaliland; Germany establishes colonies in Africa.

1885
British under Cecil Rhodes seize Bechuanaland; Germany colonizes Tanganyika in Africa.

1886
Gold discovered in the Transvaal.

1888
British occupy Uganda.

1895
Jameson raid of the Transvaal fails.

1898
British army confronts French in Nigeria; British occupy the Sudan.

1899–1902
Boer War in South Africa.

1902
Britain and Japan enter into an alliance; economist J. A. Hobson publishes *Imperialism: A Study.*

1907
Papua New Guinea taken over by British and Australians.

1914
Mohandas Gandhi returns to India from South Africa.

1914–1918
World War I.

1915
Britain promises to support independence for Arabs.

1916
Montagu Declaration promises self-government for India; *Sinn Féin* launches Easter Rising in Dublin.

1917
Balfour Declaration promises homeland for Jews in Palestine.

1919
April 13: British troops massacre Indian crowd at Amritsar.

1921
Anglo-Irish Treaty paves the way for the independence of Ireland.

1922
December 6: Britain turns over power in Ireland at Dublin Castle ceremony; Naval Treaty sets limits on British, American, and Japanese navies.

1927
All-British commission named to study reform in India.

1930
Gandhi leads salt march in India.

1931
Statute of Westminster gives independence to "white" dominions.

1932
Britain reinstates protective tariffs at Ottawa Conference.

1939–1945
World War II.

1941
Britain and the United States sign the Atlantic Charter, calling for self-determination of peoples.

1945
Labour Party wins general election; Clement Atlee replaces Winston Churchill as prime minister; Labour Party passes Colonial Development and Welfare Act; the Pan-African Congress, meeting in England, passes a resolution to seek independence.

1947
March: Lord Louis Mountbatten becomes viceroy of India.

August 14: Muslim state of Pakistan declares independence.

August 15: Hindu state of India declares independence.

November: United Nations votes to partition Palestine between Jews and Arabs.

1948
Jews in Palestine proclaim nation of Israel (May 18); Burma withdraws

from British Empire; riots in Accra spark independence movement in the Gold Coast.

1950
Kwame Nkrumah orders boycott in the Gold Coast.

1951
First general election in black Africa conducted in the Gold Coast.

1954
Britain and Egypt sign a treaty calling for British withdrawal from the Suez Canal Zone.

1956
Gamal Nasser seizes control of the Suez Canal in Egypt; Britain forced to withdraw after invasion; the Sudan becomes independent.

1957
Harold Macmillan succeeds Anthony Eden as prime minister of Britain; British begin negotiations on Cyprus after two years of guerrilla warfare; Malaysia and Ghana become independent.

1960
Cyprus becomes independent; Macmillan gives "Wind of Change" speech in South Africa.

1963
Jomo Kenyatta named prime minister of Kenya.

1967
British withdraw from Aden.

1973
Britain admitted to European Common Market.

1982
Britain goes to war with Argentina over Falkland Islands.

1997
Britain returns Hong Kong to China after ninety-nine years of British rule.

For Further Reading

Catherine Bush, *Gandhi*. New York: Chelsea House, 1985. Part of the *World Leaders Past and Present* series, this volume follows the life of Mohandas Gandhi and his struggle to bring independence to India.

Leonard Everett Fisher, *Gandhi*. New York: Atheneum, 1995. Outstanding biography for young readers on the life of Mohandas Gandhi; unusual in that it concentrates on Gandhi's career in South Africa rather than his later exploits in India.

Paul Goalen, *India*. Cambridge, England: Cambridge University Press, 1993. Covers the expansion of the Mughal Empire in India through its decline and the eventual takeover of India by the British.

Dan Larsen, *David Livingstone*. Uhrichsville, Ohio: Barbour & Co., 1996. Biography of the Scottish missionary and explorer who opened the way for the colonization of much of central Africa.

Works Consulted

Colin Cross, *The Fall of the British Empire: 1918–1968.* New York: Coward McCann, 1968. An exhaustive look at the extent of the empire just after World War I and the factors that led to its rapid decline over the next fifty years.

Edward F. Dolan Jr., *A Lion in the Sun.* New York: Parents' Magazine Press, 1973. Matter-of-fact account of the growth and eventual loss of the British Empire that does not go into great detail about the causes of its decline.

Robert Hughes, *The Fatal Shore.* New York: Alfred A. Knopf, 1987. Fascinating account of the settling of Australia by British convicts and the interaction of the British with aborigines.

Robert A. Huttenback, *The British Imperial Experience.* New York: Harper and Row, 1966. Examines the rise and fall of the British Empire not only by examining broad themes but also by focusing on specific watershed incidents such as the Indian Mutiny.

Lawrence James, *The Rise and Fall of the British Empire.* New York: St. Martin's Press, 1994. Massive and highly readable account of the empire from its beginnings in the explorations of the sixteenth century to the present day.

Paul Kennedy, *The Rise and Fall of the Great Powers.* New York: Vantage Books, 1989. Very lengthy and scholarly examination of the forces that have raised and lowered the fortunes of nations since the 1400s.

Brian Lapping, *End of Empire.* New York: St. Martin's Press, 1985. Describes the decline of the British Empire in ten widely separated possessions, including India, Palestine, Egypt, and Rhodesia.

William Manchester, *Visions of Glory.* Vol. 1 of *The Last Lion: Winston Spencer Churchill.* New York: Dell, 1983. Wonderfully readable account of Churchill's early life; author is especially good at setting the stage by describing the state of Britain and the British Empire.

P. J. Marshall, ed., *The Cambridge Illustrated History of the British Empire*. Cambridge, England: Cambridge University Press, 1996. Well-illustrated book that looks at the empire from a historical standpoint as well as at such aspects as art, architecture, economics, and government.

James Morris, *Farewell the Trumpets: An Imperial Retreat*. New York: Harcourt Brace Jovanovich, 1978. This sequel to Morris's *Pax Britannica* examines the British Empire from its apex in 1875 to the present day.

————, *Pax Britannica: The Climax of Empire*. New York: Harcourt, Brace & World, 1968. Examines the British Empire from various standpoints as of 1875, Diamond Jubilee year of Queen Victoria.

Thomas Pakenham, *The Boer War*. New York: Random House, 1994. Massive account of the war that in many ways signaled the beginning of the end of the British Empire; includes frank and critical view of British military blunders and inhumane treatment of prisoners.

Bernard Porter, *The Lion's Share*. London: Longman Group, 1975. Comprehensive account of how and when various factors came into play that led to the decline and dissolution of the British Empire.

George Woodcock, *Who Killed the British Empire?* New York: Quadrangle/New York Times Book Co., 1974. After an extensive review of the growth of the British Empire, Woodcock traces its demise from 1930 onward.

Index

Picture Credits

About the Author

William W. Lace is a native of Fort Worth, Texas. He holds a bachelor's degree from Texas Christian University, a master's from East Texas State University, and a doctorate from the University of North Texas. After working for newspapers in Baytown, Texas, and Fort Worth, he joined the University of Texas at Arlington as sports information director and later became the director of the news service. He is now executive assistant to the chancellor for the Tarrant County College District in Fort Worth. He and his wife, Laura, live in Arlington and have two children. Lace has written numerous other works for Lucent Books, one of which—*The Death Camps* in the Holocaust Library series—was selected by the New York Public Library for its 1999 Recommended Teenage Reading List.